THINKING SKILLS
THROUGHOUT THE
CURRICULUM
A Conceptual Design

by Barbara Z. Presseisen

Pi Lambda Theta, Inc.
4101 East Third Street
Bloomington, Indiana

Published by Pi Lambda Theta, Inc.
Bloomington, Indiana 47401

© 1987 Research for Better Schools
    Copyright is claimed until 1997

Published in 1987
Printed in the United States of America
94 93 92 91 90 89 88 87   8 7 6 5 4 3 2 1

Library of Congress Cataloging in Publication Data

Library of Congress Catalog Card Number: 87-60368

Presseisen, Barbara Z.
    Thinking Skills Throughout the Curriculum: A Conceptual Design

    Bibliography: p. 101

ISBN 0-9618056-0-9

to the memory of
JEAN PIAGET
who made children's thinking serious study

This publication is based upon work performed by Research for Better Schools, Inc. under contract from the National Institute of Education, Department of Education. However, the opinions expressed herein do not necessarily reflect the position or policy of the National Institute of Education, and no official endorsement by the National Institute of Education should be inferred.

CONTENTS

ILLUSTRATIONS

FIGURES

INTRODUCTION

Never has there been as serious a challenge to education as the country's current need for higher order thinking among secondary school graduates. The nation's energetic pursuit of excellence in teaching and learning has led to new perspectives about the significance of schooling, has underlined the failings of current programs, and has generated attempts to remedy existing conditions. Much has been said about increased educational standards, more testing, higher achievement, and greater improvement. Less attention has been directed toward understanding the major factors influencing student achievement and the most productive ways to pursue these factors.

A key aspect of improved schooling and the conceptual focus of this book is the development of sophisticated, autonomous thinkers in kindergarten through grade 12. The design for a thinking skills program presented here addresses the priorities in today's curriculum. It is based on current research and knowledge about implementation in public schooling and upon the premise that the development of higher order cognitive abilities are a critical part of educating all the nation's youth.

Issues related to helping students think better or learn more effectively are as old as schooling itself, but the current focus is unique in that empirical research provides bases for understanding a new rationale for cognitive improvement. Researchers from many disciplines have presented evidence that indicates that the ways students learn in specific content areas can be developed and modified.[1] These same findings can influence the way educators perceive student abilities and the way they structure schooling. Much hinges on how particular thinking skills are defined and developed, as well as on the relationships constructed between these skills and instruction in specific content areas. This comprises major aspects of the program design proposed here.

Educators must be concerned with how a thinking skills program is implemented in the classroom and throughout a district. How should the curriculum be organized for thinking instruction? What resources are needed? What are the important aspects of staff development that are key to a successful program? The design also attempts to wrangle with these issues.

There are four major sections in the design. In Chapter 1, the theoretical bases of a thinking skills program are developed and rooted in significant research literature. Underlying assumptions and program goals are examined. In Chapter 2, the program design is presented through the development of a three-level model of thinking. The nature of the various thinking processes are explored through analysis of thinking skill examples characteristic of classroom instruction. The accompanying discussion will help readers understand the design implications for teaching these thinking skills in various school subjects. In Chapter 3, instruction, staff development, subject matter integration, and program assessment are discussed in terms of the proposed design and the context of practical constraints in building a thinking skills program. Chapter 4 presents the kinds of materials and information that should be made available to educators in order to help them plan and create a classroom program based on the design. Chapter 5 suggests how the overall design can be used by practitioners who are seeking to build a sound kindergarten through grade 12 program. Applications of this design and fine tuning of responses in real school activities will determine the level of successful curriculum renewal.

---

1. John M. Belmont, Earl C. Butterfield, and Ralph P. Ferretti, "To Secure Transfer of Training Instruct Self-Management Skills," in *How and How Much Can Intelligence Be Increased*, Douglas K. Detterman and Robert J. Sternberg, eds. (Norwood, NJ: ABLEX, 1982), 147-154; Alan H. Schoenfeld, "Can Heuristics Be Taught?" in *Cognitive Process Instruction: Research on Thinking Skills*, Jack Lochhead and John Clement, eds. (Philadelphia: The Franklin Institute Press, 1979), 315-338.

THEORETICAL BASES OF A THINKING SKILLS PROGRAM

There is no academic discipline called "thinking skills." The movement that is emerging in American education in the 1980s embraces a number of academic fields and research literatures. Like the cognitive revolution in psychology, which dates back to the 1950s, the current movement focuses on the significance of human development with its related concerns of intelligence, physical and brain development, and achievement.

The advent of information systems and the development of computerized learning also influence the ways we conceive of thinking and the views we have of instruction. Much of the current interest in cognitive science stems from fascinating developments in the areas of human information processing, linguistics, and artificial intelligence that have spurred the technological renaissance.

Understanding the current thinking skills movement also requires understanding its positive view of human development. The focus is no longer on the constraints to learning and modification. As opposed to undermining the capacity of human processes, the technological revolution has made us more aware of the specialty of human performance. We appreciate more each human being's potential for becoming an expert learner. There is an emphasis, too, on the possibilities of growth through training and extended practice. Studies of child prodigies have raised questions about how all students develop expertise, what role teaching and coaching plays, and how performance in one area might enhance ability in another field.[1] The possibility of transfer provides a new functional approach to education that is positive, and, according to Beilin, stresses not only skills, strategies, rules and cognitive processes, but the role that parents, schools, and culture play in influencing cognitive development.[2] In the current thinking skills movement, there is a new emphasis on learning by doing and being involved in learning. There is a greater appreciation of the importance of early intervention to help children become better learners. The great changes that have influenced academic contributions to the development of human thought are central to understanding the bases of a particular thinking skills program.

A CHANGING VIEW OF HUMAN POTENTIAL

Interest in the learner as a thinker did not appear *de novo* in 1985, although educational research since the beginning of the twentieth century reflects historic roots in the cognitive potential of every child.[3] Albeit, this was a minority position. Traditional educational philosophy, until World War II, held that "education was a process of passing facts from those who had them to those who didn't, and pedagogy was the art or science of packaging those facts."[4]

However, after the war, awareness of child development and examinations of classroom learning led some researchers to a different view of the teacher and the student as dynamic forces in an ever changing teaching-learning system. For example, over 20 years ago, Gordon saw the Einsteinian model of the learner as the appropriate view for educational decision making.[5] The active, transactional relationships of an open system, as inspired by the great scientist, seemed to fit the newly developing behavioral science concepts and early systems theory orientation of that era: intelligence is modifiable; the child interacts with the environment and changes as a result of that interaction; the role of the teacher and the materials of instruction are significant to the quality of interaction; and the learner can use feedback to regulate better his or her own learning and, ultimately, to control that learning.

Several of the principles noted by Gordon are reiterated in the literature of the current thinking skills movement. For example, in contrast to a notion of fixed intelligence, Sternberg maintains that intelligence can be modified and that classroom experience can be organized to enhance its development.[6] He suggests that educators should concentrate on intelligence as multiple thinking and learning skills and not as static I.Q. scores, and he challenges practitioners to work actively to enhance students' reasoning capacities.

Whimbey further maintains that intelligence can be taught and suggests that instruction be focused on the multiple processes that constitute good thinking.[7] Recently, he stressed that it is the processing and reflection about the various abilities that really help the student improve his or her higher cognitive capacity. He reinforces Gordon's notion that rate and sequence of development are really influenced by the quality of awareness generated by the actual learning activity.

There are multiple instructional environments possible in schooling; the educator's task is to enable children to be active in each and to reflect on their rich experience. Such reflection may differ among youngsters, due to their unique talents and abilities, but metacognitive realizations are an important aspect in each student's learning and thinking.

Metacognition, the consciousness of one's own thought processes, is a factor that sets the current thinking skills movement apart from earlier periods of cognitive study. Becoming more aware of one's abilities and disabilities are key realizations in changing or improving intellectual capacity. Likewise, knowing how a student thinks—as expressed and performed by the student—can be the teacher's most important resource for helping to create a productive learning environment in the classroom. Mediating the metacognitive, says Costa, is the heart of teaching thinking skills.[8] Through such mediation, the teacher becomes the inspirer and the model of good thinking. Mediation, says Feuerstein, is the major task of teaching.[9]

Mediation for better thinking is also an aspect of classroom assessment. Knowing cannot merely be tested on Friday, at the end of a unit, or at the conclusion of a convenient semester. Knowing develops gradually and relates to knowledge acquired previously, as well as to the quality of experience in "playing with" that knowledge. Thus, the ways thinking skills are defined in any subject area and the ways students acquire proficiency in handling particular cognitive difficulties becomes quite significant to their mastery of particular content. In applying a concern for thinking to the traditional subjects of schooling, there is much that we can learn from comparing the growing proficiency of a novice to the honed skills of the more mature or successful learner. Chall, Larkin, and Schoenfeld discuss awareness in their respective subject areas of reading, science, and mathematics.[10] In each area, there is a growing complexity of information and an increasing abstractness of process. Therefore, when textbook material is weak in depicting higher cognitive operations and how they are developed for student learning, teachers experience frustration in attempting to use such texts to parallel their higher level instruction.[11]

The emerging view of human potential leans toward differing definitions of human intelligence. Gardner proposes seven intelligences and raises questions about which subjects should be included in the curriculum and with what degree of emphasis.[12] If certain thinking processes underlie all disciplines or pertain to certain intelligences, aren't these significant organizing centers for curriculum? In addition, how best can culture, technology, and intellect interrelate instructionally? Olson suggests that the world's multiple symbol systems exist to be tapped by the learner's intelligences.[13] However, most schools fail to develop or use these various systems. Basic skills programs cater to linguistic and quantitative learning modalities in simplistic ways. Are we failing to develop human potential more broadly? Several leaders of the thinking skills movement maintain that we are and even suggest that the inability and failure of many students may stem from such a narrow approach. Some advocate that by gradual reinforcement and careful reiteration, students can become fluent in rediscovering redundant rules that are imbedded in new content and thereby become more fluent in a specific operation.[14]

Finally, there is a notion in the more current view of human potential that there may be optimal times for particular learning. The research on child development, which spans from Piaget's studies after World War I to the recent Perry Preschool program study, and current research on adolescence and formal reasoning suggest that particular periods in the learner's development are key to certain cognitive experiences and should be maximized in the design of instruction.[15] This is not to say that the same experiences are important for all children at the same instructional moment, but the sequence of cognitive change and the quality of experience parallel to the learner's involvement and understanding are important considerations in planning the long-range school curriculum. A program design for teaching thinking must be concerned with this developmental concern, and ultimately it must relate it to the plan for classroom instruction, as well as to the organization of program content.

A CHANGING VIEW OF INSTRUCTION
AND THE INSTRUCTIONAL PROGRAM

As views of human potential change, other views of instruction and the instructional program also emerge. These views stem from the more active characterization of the learner and from a more complete understanding of the instructional process itself. Bruner describes five models to depict the young learner.[16] Three of these models touch on expectations of the current thinking skills movement. A learner characterized as a *hypothesis generator* exhibits the active curiosity thinking skill educators hope to find in the classroom. Information is manipulated freely, and one right answer does not dominate instruction. The learner characterized as *constructor of knowledge* is self-reliant and gradually masters the rules of knowledge development. This student builds autonomy or independence and self-management skills. The *novice-to-expert* learner emphasizes pragmatic learning and the efficiency of specificity and explicitness. He or she learns from a coaching instructor and knows the value of practice.

In designing a thinking skills program, educators must deal inevitably with the model of the learning process itself, for this becomes the basis of instruction. In analyzing specific published thinking skills programs, Campione and Armbruster question which organizational framework is most appropriate for exploring learning in the classroom.[17] The scheme they devise has four dimensions (see Figure 1).

The characteristics of the learner are obviously important and include the level of individual skill, the amount and quality of prior knowledge, and particular values and attitudes that might affect learning. Criterial tasks, the processes most involved in thinking, are a second consideration. The particular activities associated with learning are stressed. Finally, the nature of the educational materials themselves—how they are presented, and what they are capable of inspiring—plays an important role in stimulating interaction among students and teachers in the instructional process.

From this model of learning, instruction designed to enhance student thinking skills would emphasize conditions that are different from those that have been stressed in the traditional classroom. First, the teacher's role would not be portrayed as the fount of all wisdom, a lecturing informer, or the sole repository of knowledge. The teacher as facilitator or model, occasionally as critic, and always as motivator, may teach from the back of the classroom, in the school's resource center, and in the community at large.[18] Covering content would be less important than explication of process, raising novel questions, or determining the cause of student error.

The context of the classroom as an environment for learning also needs to be considered. Thinking classrooms are busy places. They may be noisy. It is likely that students will be grouped according to their learning needs, encouraged to be proud of and responsible for their own work and seek autonomy in learning as well as work cooperatively in groups of peers. Testing would be designed to help figure out concepts that students don't understand, to locate the sources of misconception, and to relate as closely as possible to the content of the subject matter and to the processes associated with learning it.

What would the curriculum be like in a thinking and learning skills classroom? Eisner suggests that it should be "a mind-altering device."[19] Sizer advocates that it is subject matter that "should lead somewhere, in the eyes and mind of the student."[20] He stresses that curriculum should relate ideas meaningfully. The thinking skills classrooms should also become centers for pursu-

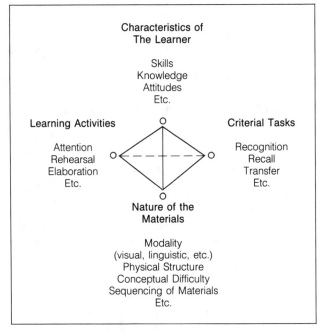

FIGURE 1: An Organizational Framework for
Exploring Questions About Learning

From Acquiring information from texts: An analysis of four ap- proaches (p. 332) by J. C. Campione & B. B. Armbruster. In J. W. Segal, S.F. Chipman, & R. Glaser (Eds.), 1985, Thinking and Learning Skills (Vol. 1), Hillsdale, NJ: Lawrence Erlbaum As- sociates. Reprinted by permission of Lawrence Erlbaum As- sociates.

ing information and knowledge. The thinking skills curriculum and the related strategies of learning ought to enable motivated students to find the best match of task, information, and skill, and then create for themselves an understanding and a personal meaning of the world around them. The expert's knowledge and ability might help the learner focus his or her thoughts more exactly, but for that wonderful moment of realization and mastery, the learner is the actual inventor or scholar, and the classroom needs to facilitate that experience.

Today's emphasis on thinking changes the focus of instruction and teachers' orientation to it. In charting the curriculum's course, teachers face the awesome task of pulling together the appropriate mix of material, activity, and skill for each student's progress. Time and space have been enlarged in this new relationship. Teachers should be concerned with the important teaching moment, but not just in one classroom and not just for the current academic year. Professionals in the school need to discuss each child's long-range, developmental performance, plan a multi-year program, and select materials across several grade levels, all oriented to a common understanding of what academic achievement ought to be and become for the school's population. Several of the new thinking skills programs assume that collegial interaction among staff is a requisite to and a necessity for program development. There is an underlying assumption that teachers are professional and must have the autonomy to make professional decisions about learning and the curriculum. There is a further assumption in the current movement that both building and central office leadership seek to foster this kind of decision-making relationship.

The current thinking skills movement presents a re-ordering of relationships in education (see Figure 2). At the heart is the teaching process, the teacher's action that mediates between the learner and that portion of the environment to be learned. The curriculum is the grist for the teaching mill. Both teaching and curriculum are part of a larger instructional design, which is concerned with pedagogical methods, the logical interaction with other learners, and even the interrelationships among various contents and meanings across many years of study. Here is where metacognitive concerns are at work and the gradual building of cognitive operations into complex schemes of subject matter knowledge takes place. Reif speaks about how the learner supplants earlier notions with more adequate concepts as complex cognitive schemas are built.[21] He also suggests that it may be necessary to explicitly and systematically teach these methods by careful design, if we want them to develop. Finally, schooling—the total of the learner's educational experience that is rooted in high expectations and reliant on a qualitative educational climate—surrounds the other dimensions and sets the tone for the entire school program. At this level, the role of school leadership, staff development, and the ongoing influence of building and central office support are most keenly felt.

BASIC ASSUMPTIONS OF A THINKING SKILLS PROGRAM THROUGHOUT THE CURRICULUM

The foregoing theoretical considerations lead to several basic assumptions, which are the underpinnings of a thinking skills program for K-12 curriculum. The following assumptions serve as the guiding principles of program development in the proposed design:

- instruction and curriculum focused on intellectual abilities, embodied in basic and advanced cognitive processes that develop throughout a student's experience at school
- basic and advanced cognitive processes defined and employed as thinking skills in instructional decision making
- continuous examination of these cognitive processes and their depiction in the presentation of specific contents, as well as related to the rules of more complex content formation
- varied instructional contexts and learner modalities in applications of the several cognitive processes
- development of student intellectual autonomy and more efficient self-monitoring of cognitive performance

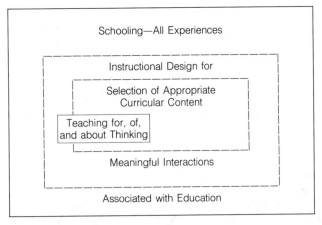

FIGURE 2: Educational Relationships in the School

- improvement of classroom activities and organization (individual and group) to enhance cognitive experiences at all grade levels
- development of assessments, including tests appropriate for cognitive development, and diagnostic use of results of such examinations for planning better instructional activities
- a focus on optimal learning periods—early childhood's initial presentation and early adolescence, when there is a shift to higher order operations
- use of the best materials and media for developing various cognitive operations
- planning and implementation of staff development programs and technical support efforts that help teachers and administrators jointly focus on thinking skills instruction and program development.

These guidelines and the research from which they are drawn are the bases for the program design described in Chapter 2.

---

1. David H. Feldman, "Piaget on Giftedness—A Very Short Essay," *The Genetic Epistemologist* 12 (1983): 1-10.

2. Harry Beilin, "The Psychology of Mathematics Learning," *Education and Urban Society* 17 (1985): 377-385.

3. John Dewey, *Experience in Education* (London: Collier-Macmillan, 1938); Jean Piaget, in *Piaget's Theory in Carmichael's Manual of Child Psychology*, vol. 1, Paul H. Mussen, ed. (New York: John Wiley, 1970), 703-732; Jerome Bruner, *On Knowing: Essays for the Left Hand* (New York: Atheneum, 1967).

4. Jack Lochhead, "Introduction to Section 1—New Horizons in Educational Development," in *Review of Research in Education*, vol. 12, Edmund W. Gordon, ed. (Washington, D.C.: American Educational Research Association, 1985), 4.

5. Ira J. Gordon, *Studying the Child in School* (New York: John Wiley, 1966).

6. Robert J. Sternberg, "Intelligence as Thinking and Learning Skills," *Educational Leadership* 39 (1981): 18-20; Sternberg, "How Can We Teach Intelligence?" *Educational Leadership* 42 (1984): 38-48; Sternberg, "What Should Intelligence Tests Test? Implications of a Triarchic Theory of Intelligence for Intelligence Testing." *Educational Researcher* 13 (1984): 5-15.

7. Arthur A. Whimbey and Linda S. Whimbey, *Intelligence Can Be Taught* (New York: E.P. Dutton, 1975).

8. Arthur L. Costa, "Mediating the Metacognitive," *Educational Leadership* 42 (1984): 57-62.

9. Reuven Feuerstein, *Instrumental Enrichment: An Intervention Program for Cognitive Modifiability* (Baltimore: University Park Press, 1980); Reuven Feuerstein et al., "Instrumental Enrichment, an Intervention Program for Structural Cognitive Modifiability: Theory and Practice," in *Thinking and Learning Skills*, vol. 1,

Judith W. Segal, Susan F. Chipman, and Robert Glaser, eds. (Hillsdale, NJ: Lawrence Erlbaum Associates, 1985).

10. Jeanne S. Chall, *Stages of Reading Development* (New York: McGraw-Hill, 1983); Jean Osborn, Beau F. Jones, Marcy Stein, "The Case for Improving Textbooks," *Educational Leadership* 42 (1985): 9-16; Jill H. Larkin, "Teaching Problem Solving in Physics: The Psychological Laboratory and the Practical Classroom," in *Problem Solving and Education: Issues in Teaching and Research*, David T. Tuma and Frederick Reif, eds. (Hillsdale, NJ: Lawrence Erlbaum Associates, 1980), 111-115; Alan H. Schoenfeld, "Teaching Problem-Solving Skills." *The American Mathematical Monthly* 87 (1980): 794-805.

11. Robert F. Nicely, Jr., "Higher Order Thinking Skills in Mathematics Textbooks," *Educational Leadership* 42 (1985): 26-30.

12. Howard Gardner, *Frames of Mind: The Theory of Multiple Intelligences* (New York: Basic Books, 1983).

13. David R. Olson, "What is Worth Knowing and What Can Be Taught?" *School Review* 82 (1973): 27-43; Olson, "Culture, Technology, and Intellect," in *The Nature of Intelligence*, Lauren B. Resnick, ed. (Hillsdale, NJ: Lawrence Erlbaum Associates, 1976); Olson, "Computers as Tools of the Intellect," *Educational Researcher* 14 (1985): 5-7.

14. Reuven Feuerstein et al., "Instrumental Enrichment," 1985, 60.

15. John R. Berrueta-Clement et al., *Changed Lives: The Effects of the Perry Preschool Program on Youths Through Age 19* (Ypsilanti, MI: High/Scope Press, 1984); John R. Mergendoller, "To Facilitate or Impede? The Impact of Selected Organizational Features of Secondary Schools on Adolescent Development" (Paper delivered at the Invitational Conference on Adolescence and Secondary Schooling, University of Wisconsin Research and Development Center, 7-10 November 1981); David Elkind, "The View of David Elkind," in *The Development of Adolescent Thinking: Some Views for Effective Schools*, Barbara Z. Presseisen, ed. (Philadelphia, PA: Research for Better Schools, 1983), 23-28; Albert Benderson, "Growing Up Is Hard to Do," *ETS Developments* 31 (1985): 5-8.

16. Jerome Bruner, "Models of the Learner," *Educational Researcher* 14 (1985): 5-8.

17. Joseph C. Campione and Bonnie B. Armbruster, "Acquiring Information from Texts: An Analysis of Four Approaches," in *Thinking and Learning Skills*, vol. 1, Judith W. Segal, Susan F. Chipman, and Robert Glaser, eds. (Hillsdale, NJ: Lawrence Erlbaum Associates, 1985).

18. Costa, "Mediating the Metacognitive."

19. Elliot W. Eisner, "Creative Education in American Schools Today" *educational HORIZONS* 63 (Special Edition, 1985): 10-15.

20. Theodore Sizer, *Horace's Compromise: The Dilemma of the American High School* (Boston: Houghton Mifflin, 1984), 1110.

21. Frederick Reif, "Teaching Higher-Order Thinking Skills for a Technological World: Needs and Opportunities" (Paper prepared for the American Educational Research Association Project: Research Contributions for Educational Improvement, November, 1984).

2

PROGRAM DESIGN

Thinking and learning skills form the heart of a school's program. In order to arrive at a substantive basis on which to design a challenging curriculum, educators should seek answers to the following questions:

1. Which thinking and learning skills should be included in a kindergarten through grade 12 curriculum?
2. How should these thinking and learning skills be defined? Should they be presented in a specific order?
3. How should these thinking and learning skills be sequenced across various grade levels?
4. How are students' developing abilities accounted for in the sequence?
5. How are these thinking and learning skills related to existing courses or subject matters?
6. How can these thinking and learning skills be developed in actual classroom lessons and related student activities?
7. How are these thinking and learning skills characterized in various student assessments, including both classroom and standardized testing?

These questions represent the significant issues in the initial development of a thinking skills program. Although current research may not be available to respond fully to all of them, practitioners should continue to pursue the answers through commitment

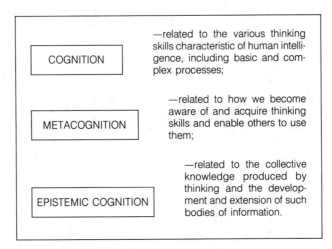

FIGURE 3. A Tri-Level Model of Thinking

to an actual program. Ultimately, implementation will provide practical experience that will enlighten basic theory.

A program design for teaching thinking requires a basic concept that is rich enough to account for complex human thought processes. A three-level working model of thinking, based on work in cognition and on earlier discussions of thinking and learning, is presented here (see Figure 3).[1] It is not intended as a prescription, but as a tentative taxonomy consistent with current research. It is a framework in which to ground practical decisions.

In the model presented, the first level refers to the essential and complex cognitive processes that underlie the student's thinking. Skills such as classifying, reasoning, and generalizing are frequently associated with academic learning. In addition, much of the current literature on thinking stresses the significance of higher order processes like problem solving, creative and critical thinking. For a model to be useful, it must define both these types of skills or processes. It also must indicate how these cognitive operations relate to one another, and how best to approach them in a curriculum that focuses on successful student mastery.

The second level of the model addresses the metacognitive processes that are influential in helping the student learn to work with initial skills. What awarenesses are important to improve performance? Are there routines that all learners can develop to assist them in the instructional task? How do skilled performers refine or even invent new routines? How do these processes develop over the 13 years of a student's public school career? The model must also help explicate the metacognitive processes, indicate how these processes are related to one another, and provide guidance relevant to their conscious development across the long-term curriculum.

The program design generated from the three-level model of thinking will also touch on epistemic considerations, those relationships bound by the nature of the content disciplines. But the main thrust, in terms of application to elementary and secondary teaching, is the *development* of cognitive and metacognitive processes. The following sections seek to explicate this three-level model of thinking and relate it further to the organization of an overall curricular design.

COGNITION: Definition of Essential Thinking Skills

There is no agreed-upon taxonomy of basic thinking skills. The fact that the developmental stages of a learner's cognitive ability always interact with the learner's actual thinking performance is but one of the key perspectives to understanding which processes are essential building blocks of children's thought. The first question in constructing a curriculum model is, What are the *cognitive* processes themselves?

The learner's basic or essential thinking skills can be divided into five major categories which are organized according to increasing complexity and abstractness: qualification, classification, relationships, transformations, and causation. Figure 4 suggests a continuum of groups of skills or processes that might appear as the student works with various subject matters. The exactness of any one process is not important, although the definitions of the skills are crucial to providing common meanings to teachers and students about thinking. What is important is the kind of *cognitive operation* embedded in each category of thinking. These are the mental manipulations that students learn to perform as they try to make sense of academic tasks. They learn these manipulations in varying contexts, as well as in differing modalities—verbal, quantitative, spatial, figural, and symbolic. A thinking skills program's primary purpose is to ensure that students learn to perform the various skills of each category in appropriate tasks through various subject matters and with increasing complexity. This will assure not only that the learner finds meaning in the instructional task, but that the learning pertains to fluency in a variety of cognitive skills and to a developmentally appropriate accumulation of these skills. Some thinking skills programs are organized to do just that. They will be discussed later.

- **QUALIFICATION** — finding unique characteristics

  units or basic identity;
  definitions; specific facts;
  problem/task recognition

- **CLASSIFICATION** — determining common qualities

  similarities and differences; correspondence;
  grouping and sorting; comparisons;
  either/or distinctions;
  typologies

- **RELATIONSHIPS** — detecting regular operations

  parts and wholes; numerical progressions; patterns;
  sequences and order; hierarchy; prioritization;
  logical deductions; generalizations

- **TRANSFORMATIONS** — relating known to unknown;
  creating new meanings

  analogies;
  metaphors; idioms;
  logical inductions; translations;
  applications; hypotheses

- **CAUSATION** — establishing cause and effect,
  interpretation; predictions;
  forecasting

  inferences;
  judgments;
  evaluations; assessment;

Increasing Complexity and Abstractness

FIGURE 4. A Model of Essential Thinking Skills:
Basic Processes

The following examples of specific items that tap particular thinking skill categories illustrate these basic processes. Discussion is provided to indicate how the particular example relates to the larger questions of curricular design.

Qualification is the depiction of the unique characteristic of the idea or concept involved in learning. The primary function of such a skill is definitional, establishing, as shown here, the key aspects of being *triangular*. Much learning depends on a clear understanding of the object of instruction. What is a *prime number*? What does it mean to be a *citizen*? What is the *weight* of an object? Building a skill of qualification develops discriminating abilities and enlarges the learner's capacities to be explicit and exact.

Although there is a comparison involved in II,1, the task can-

I. QUALIFICATION: Example 1

A *triangle* is a figure that looks like one of these:

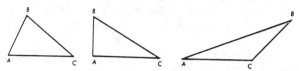

From Geometry, *p. 84, by Edwin E. Moise and Floyd L. Downs, Jr. (Menlo Park, CA: Addison Wesley, 1975), reprinted by permission of Addison Wesley.*

II. CLASSIFICATION: Example 1

Which drawing (a,b,c, or d) is the same as the one at left?

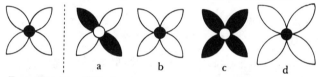

a   b   c   d

From "Thinking Skills," *p. 87, by Richard W. Samson, in* Strategic Reasoning, *John J. Glade, ed. (Stamford, CT: Innovative Sciences, 1982), reprinted by permission of Innovative Sciences, Inc.*

not be completed unless the unique qualities of the item on the left are first established in the student's mind. More complex thinking processes often require the student to move backward to elementary skills in order to arrive at a correct solution. Similarly, basic elements often build up to more complex operations or are extended to more encompassing instances. For example, elementary school youngsters may learn the definition of a homonym as words that sound alike but have different meanings and different spellings. Examples can be generated: *mail/male; sun/son; there/their.* In the third example, the word *they're* could also be introduced, but might confuse the thinker unless the basic qualification is again checked. Does this example fit the definition?, the teacher might query. If so, how? The question causes the student to reexamine the initial qualification.

Making the comparisons needed in classifications often requires the learner to examine and re-examine primary data: How do these things go together? What are the ways these items are alike or different? These are questions that extend the discrimination of the first category to more intricate relationships, or, at least to momentary likenesses or differences to be noted and retained.

Sometimes the comparison requires mental manipulation of the evidence, as illustrated in II,4.

Also illustrated in this example is the possibility that one problem may have multiple correct responses. Testing in most instances dwells on the notion of only one correct response. Teaching for more powerful thinking may need to encourage students to think in terms of several alternative answers, depending on supportive conditions and constraints.

When items are related in consistent and regular ways, patterns emerge. Sometimes these relationships may not be obvious immediately and require the student to step back to a categorization task. In other instances, the pattern may be built upon a rule relationship, as in alphabetical sequence or in a repeated pattern such as a musical scale. Arguments of deductive logic extend such rules to intricate relationships based on assumed premises.

II. CLASSIFICATION: Example 2

"Bob can have the ball *or* the truck. Mark what Bob can have."

From Developing Cognitive Abilities Test: Teacher's Manual, *p. 10, by John W. Wick and Jeffrey K. Smith (Iowa City, Iowa: American Testronics, 1980), reprinted by permission of American Testronics.*

II. CLASSIFICATION: Example 3

Exercise: Choose one word in each line that is a synonym and one that is an antonym of the first word.

1. slim: balance, chubby, select, thin, shrewd
2. large: small, great, unique, brutal, arbitrary
3. new: exciting, ancient, small, modern, precious
4. brave: high, orderly, craven, courageous, strange
5. smart: dull, pleasant, clever, clear, agreeable

From Our Language Today, *p. 290, by David A. Conlin et al. (Lexington, MA: D.C. Heath and Company, 1970), reprinted by permission of D.C. Heath and Company.*

II. CLASSIFICATION: Example 4

What object (a,b,c, or d) is the same as the one at left?

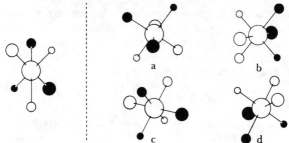

From "Thinking Skills," p. 123, by Richard W. Samson, in Strategic Reasoning, *John J. Glade, ed. (Stamford, CT: Innovative Sciences, 1982), reprinted by permission of Innovative Sciences, Inc.*

III. RELATIONSHIPS: Example 1

Which answer choice (a,b, or c) goes in the blank space?

OXXOXXOXX_____OXXOXX   OXX   OXO   XXO
                           a   b   c

From "Thinking Skills," p. 87, by Richard W. Samson, in Strategic Reasoning, *John J. Glade, ed. (Stamford, CT: Innovative Sciences, 1982), reprinted by permission of Innovative Sciences, Inc.*

III. RELATIONSHIPS: Example 2

Put these words in alphabetical order:

1. strenuous	6. steadfast	11. straight
2. stubble	7. strait	12. struggle
3. structure	8. strengthen	13. stealthy
4. style	9. stalactite	14. stalagmite
5. statue	10. stupendous	15. stationery

From Our Language Today, *p. 10, by David A. Conlin et al. (Lexington, MA: D.C. Heath and Company, 1970), reprinted by permission of D.C. Heath and Company.*

Sequence can also be a function of time and require the student to determine pattern in temporal order. Obviously, younger students may be able to deal with tasks of this sort that are close to personal experience, as in III,3, but not be able to make the associations that call for historical relationships, as presented in

III,4. The developmental sophistication of the learner is an important consideration in determining appropriate relationships to study.

In numerical progression, possible solutions may be dealt with best by having the student analyze backwards to determine the necessary next number in a sequence. Other types of numerical relationships may also involve reasoning back and forth across the problem space (see examples III, 6, 7).

III. RELATIONSHIPS: Example 3

Tester: "Mark the picture that shows how the wood looked *after* it was cut."

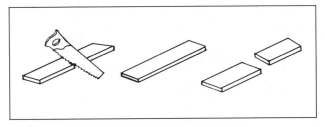

Reproduced by permission from the BOEHM TEST OF BASIC CONCEPTS. *Copyright © 1967-1970, 1971 by the Psychological Corporation. All rights reserved.*

III. RELATIONSHIPS: Example 4

Put the names on time chart where each belongs.

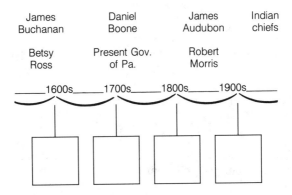

From All about Pennsylvania, *p. 56, by Lucille Wallower and Ellen J. Wholey (Harrisburg, PA: Penns Valley Publishing,1984), reprinted by permission of Penns Valley Publishers.*

III. RELATIONSHIPS: Example 5

Which answer choice (a,b,c, or d) completes the box at left?

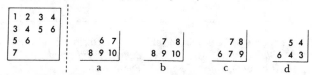

| a | b | c | d |

From "Thinking Skills," *p. 118, by Richard W. Samson, in* Strategic Reasoning, *John J. Glade, ed. (Stamford, CT: Innovative Sciences, 1982), reprinted by permission of Innovative Sciences, Inc.*

III. RELATIONSHIPS: Example 6

(1) Jerry says that these two statements together sort of "add up" to a third statement. What do you think it is?

(a) I have two United States coins with a total value of 15 cents.

(b) The first coin is a dime.

(c) _____

From Discovery in Mathematics: Student Discussion Guide, *p. 50, by Robert B. Davis (New Rochelle, NY: Cuisenaire Co., 1980), reprinted by permission of the Cuisenaire Company.*

III. RELATIONSHIP: Example 7

Students are asked to circle groups of numbers that add up to 10. All the numbers must be used in contingent *(fenced)* groupings.

FENCE ARITHMETIC

```
┌─ ┬─ ┬─ ┬─ ┐
│ 5 │ 4 │ 6 │ 4 │
├─ ┼─ ┼─ ┼─ ┤
│ │ │ 5 │ 5 │ 4 │
├─ ┼─ ┼─ ┼─ ┤
│ 8 │ │ │ 2 │ 3 │
├─ ┼─ ┼─ ┼─ ┤
│ 2 │ 4 │ 4 │ 2 │
└─ ┴─ ┴─ ┴─ ┘
```

____ (10s)

From Individualized Computation, *vol. d1, p. 22, by Robert W. Wirtz (Washington, DC: Curriculum Development Associates, n.d.), reprinted by permission of Curriculum Development Associates.*

III. RELATIONSHIPS: Example 8

G-24 government, judge, president, senator

WHOLE_____PARTS_____, _____, _____

From Building Thinking Skills, bk. 1, , p. *216, by Howard and Sandra Black (Pacific Grove, CA: Midwest Publications, n.d.), reprinted by permission of Midwest Publications.*

The student needs to understand how finite parts are but a piece of the whole expressed in the overall mathematical problem. Having a view of the total task may help the student see the significance of the smaller operation, which he or she must manipulate in bringing about a solution. In other subject areas, like social studies, knowing the relationship between parts and wholes may help the student understand how the entities interact in their particular jobs and responsibilities, as the next example illustrates.

Spatial relationships depicting time or quantity may help to detect regular operations. Timelines in history and geographical map grids aid students in pursuing these relationships. For example, in the Relative Position and Motion Unit of the Science Curriculum Improvement Study (SCIS) program, students are told the coordinates on a rectangular grid map and are asked to name the specific places designated. Next, the students are told specific

III. RELATIONSHIPS: Example 9

1. For the sake of argument, accept each of the following hypotheses and then give a logical completion for each conclusion.

   (a) Hypothesis: All boys like to play football. My brother is fourteen years old.
   Conclusion: My brother _____.

   (b) Hypothesis: Only careless people make mistakes. I am never careless.
   Conclusion: I_____.

   (c) Hypothesis: Jack always laughs when he tells a joke. Jack is telling a joke.
   Conclusion: Jack _____.

   (d) Hypothesis: In an isosceles triangle, the base angles are congruent.
   In $\triangle$ ABC, AC = BC.
   Conclusion: _____.

From Geometry, p. *179, by Edwin E. Moise and Floyd L. Downs, Jr. (Menlo Park, CA: Addison Wesley, 1975), reprinted by permission of Addison Wesley.*

places and are asked to tell the coordinate units. The purpose is to point out that location is a relative concept contingent on exact information about spatial and quantifiable relationships.[2]

The student can be introduced to making logical deductions about regular relationships. Given basic information that is constant in occurrence, the student can conclude certain results. A science class, for instance, could trace the development of Mendelian genetics and the potential heredity of subsequent generations in terms of particular knowledge about the parental group. By knowing the possible combinations of genetic traits, students can deduce the outcome of regularly occurring relationships and anticipate the likelihood of their occurrence in the genetic hierarchy. Where relationships are not constant, or intervening information suggests that patterns will not be upheld, students can come to realize that certain conditions must be met for hypotheses to work accurately.

IV. TRANSFORMATIONS: Example 1

From Developing Cognitive Abilities Test: Teacher's Manual, *p. 10, by John W. Wick and Jeffrey K. Smith (Iowa City, Iowa: American Testronics, 1980), reprinted by permission of American Testronics.*

Recognizing simple analogies is rooted in the grouping and sorting tasks that are part of the classification category. Students can begin by working on items that use familiar contexts and simpler language structures.

IV. TRANSFORMATIONS: Example 2

Circle the right word to finish each sentence.

1. **Toothache** is to **jaw** as **headache** is to. . . .
   a. health   b. thought   c. head

2. **Baseball** is to **field** as **basketball** is to. . . .
   a. street   b. court   c. backboard

3. **Leader** is to **group** as **chief** is to. . . .
   a. tribe   b. learn   c. class

4. **Week** is to **month** as **month** is to. . . .
   a. day   b. year   c. midnight

From Basic Goals in Spelling, *6th edition, Level 4, p. 56, by William Kottmayer and Audrey Claus. Copyright © 1980 by McGraw-Hill Book Company, Webster Division. Used with permission of McGraw-Hill.*

IV. TRANSFORMATIONS: Example 3

$$\frac{RENT}{MONTH} = \frac{GASOLINE}{\quad} \quad \vert \quad GALLON \quad VOLUME \quad VOLATILE$$

$$\vert \qquad a \qquad b \qquad \quad c$$

From "Thinking Skills," p. 116, by Richard W. Samson, in Strategic Reasoning, John J. Glade, ed. (Stamford, CT: Innovative Sciences, 1982), reprinted by permission of Innovative Sciences, Inc.

Eventually, the examples get more complicated because differing kinds of relationships become significant. In more difficult analogies, the student must generate rules for hidden dimensions within the analogy. The rules form new meanings for the learner and suggest how the answer has to be related to the example. There may be as many as 15 types of relationships involved in analogy building.

1.	synonyms	−generous : liberal
2.	antonyms	−never : always
3.	symbol	−cross : Christianity
4.	worker : tool	−author : pen
5.	worker : product	−author : novel
6.	class : species	−mammal : man
7.	part : whole	−pupil : class
8.	function	−bell : rings
9.	cause	−germ : disease
10.	size	−village : city
11.	surplus	−flood : water
12.	lack	−invalid : health
13.	place	−swimming : pond
14.	sex	−duck : drake
15.	description	−snail : slow

From Junior English Review Exercises Book 1, p. 15, by Earl F. Wood (Cambridge, MA: Educators Publishing Service, 1979), reprinted by permission of Educators Publishing Service.

Exploring with language may involve the kinds of transformation in creating metaphors. Consider the following example:

IV. TRANSFORMATIONS: Example 4

A concept may be thought of in terms of many different metaphors. For example:

Memory is an attic.
Memory is a fishing net.
Memory is a refrigerator.

How else might we think of memory? Think of several additional ways.

Memory is _____?_____.

From "Thinking Skills," p. 138, by Richard W. Samson, in Strategic Reasoning, *John J. Glade, ed. (Stamford, CT: Innovative Sciences, 1982), reprinted by permission of Innovative Sciences, Inc.*

IV. TRANSFORMATIONS: Example 5

EXERCISE: Choose ten of the idioms below and make a drawing or cartoon to illustrate the literal meaning of each of the expressions. Under each drawing, write a sentence that conveys the same idea but uses different words. Try to avoid slang expressions or idioms in your sentences. Have your classmates guess which expressions you have represented.

1. that's not my bag	8. too many irons in the fire
2. he blew it	9. pulling my leg
3. it bugs me	10. let the cat out of the bag
4. laughing his head off	11. working to beat the band
5. lose your cool	12. throw in the sponge
6. feeling his oats	13. egging him on
7. being flat broke	14. call on the carpet

From Our Language Today, *p. 20, by David A. Conlin et al. (Lexington, MA: D.C. Heath and Company, 1970), reprinted by permission of D.C. Heath Company.*

Exploring idioms enables students to discover implicit meaning in words and ways of not meaning what you say. Transformations involve a kind of translation process, as in the reading of dialect shown in the Irish-American version of the nursery rhyme *Mary Had a Little Lamb*, illustrated in IV,6.

IV. TRANSFORMATIONS: Example 6

IV

Begorry, Mary had a little shape,
And the wool was white entoirely.
An' wherever Mary wad sthir her sthumps
The young shape would follow her completely.

From Our Language Today, *p. 19, by David A. Conlin et al. (Lexington, MA: D.C. Heath and Company, 1970), reprinted by permission of D.C. Heath and Company.*

IV. TRANSFORMATIONS: Example 7

INVESTIGATING FURTHER

Set up a lever like the one shown in the diagram. You will need a pint milk carton, some sand or soil, a ruler to be used as a lever, a spring scale, and perhaps a wooden block as the fulcrum. Use the carton filled with sand as your load. You can apply an effort to lift the load by pulling down on the lever.

Keep the fulcrum in the same location all the time. Change the weight of the load by adding or pouring out sand. Will there also be a change in the amount of effort you have to use?

Find out whether the change in load corresponds in any way to the change in effort. You can weigh the load each time by using your spring scale. Write down your results after each trial.

From Concepts in Science, *Third Edition, by Paul Brandwein et al., copyright © 1972 by Harcourt Brace Jovanovich, Inc. Reprinted by permission of the publisher.*

Finally, the student can use experimental situations as analogous exploratory tasks. By altering conditions, new information can be generated about the relationships among the various parts of the experiments. By organizing the emergent results of the experiment, rules can be generated relative to possible constants or consistent patterns. The basis for establishing causal effects is laid and a new thinking category is reached. The student is able to say, "If these situations pertain to these materials, then this happens. . . ." A new level of thinking is achieved. Simpler skills become the more complex processes of higher order reasoning and problem solving.

Causation involves verifiable assessments or evaluations.

V. CAUSATION: Example 1

7. The concept that fits the main concept of this section is
   a. Friction is a force that has no usefulness.
   b. The amount of friction depends on the kinds of surfaces that are in contact.

From Concepts in Science, *Third Edition, by Paul Brandwein et al., copyright © 1972 by Harcourt Brace Jovanovich, Inc. Reprinted by permission of the publisher.*

V. CAUSATION: Example 2

If the present sequence continues, what will the remainder of the graph look like?

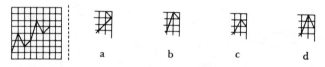

a   b   c   d

From "Thinking Skills," p. 122, by Richard W. Samson, in Strategic Reasoning, John J. Glade, ed. (Stamford, CT: Innovative Sciences, 1982), reprinted by permission of Innovative Sciences, Inc.

There are controlling reasons why particular relationships are so: the proofs in geometric solution, interpreting a writer's implications in a particular passage, determining a juror's decision about a prisoner's guilt or innocence as related to technical evidence presented.

When students determine why something is so, and give evidence of such proof, they can make inferences about conditions that will cause similar results to occur. Thus, students can be asked to predict outcomes in stories, given only the initial circumstances. Completing the plot of a novel, writing the final act for a play, or forecasting economic conditions can challenge the imagination of a youngster and test his or her powers of judgment, perception, and prediction. In doing so, basic thinking skills move to more complex and sophisticated levels of thought.

COGNITION: Definition of Complex Thinking Skills

There is a great deal of confusion about which mental processes are complex and the purposes of each process. This design proposes four complex processes, based on the essential skills, to be included in the curriculum: problem solving, decision making, critical thinking, and creative thinking. It is proposed that the four processes in Figure 5 represent distinctly different tasks.

Problem Solving

Today's emphasis on problem solving in the discussion of thinking skills draws a clear distinction between rote learning and learning with understanding. The better problem solver not only works hard at what he or she does, but does it with understanding. Simon points out that the better problem solver works at carefully structuring the problem and at clearly representing it.[3]

HIGHER ORDER SKILL	TASK	ESSENTIAL SKILLS	YIELDS
PROBLEM SOLVING	Resolve a known difficulty	Relationships Transformations Causations	Solution Conclusion Generalization (potentially)
DECISION MAKING	Choose a best alternative	Classifications Relationships	Response Best alternative
CRITICAL THINKING	Understand particular meanings	Relationships Transformations Causation	Sound reasons proof, theory
CREATIVE THINKING	Create novel or aesthetic ideas/ products	Qualification Relationships Transformations	New meanings, pleasing products

FIGURE 5. A Model of Advanced Thinking Skills: Complex Process

Information from memory, both short- and long-term, is utilized more effectively. The better problem solver works extensively at making operations explicit and seeking to understand various relational constraints. It seems that a great part of powerful problem solving is developing coping strategies where no known recipes exist. Rubinstein proposes a list of ten heuristics:

1. Get the total picture; don't get lost in detail.
2. Withhold judgment; don't commit yourself too early.
3. Create models to simplify the problems, using words, pictorial representations, symbols, or equations.
4. Try changing the representation of the problem.
5. State questions verbally; vary the form of the question.
6. Be flexible; question the credibility of your premises.
7. Try working backwards.
8. Proceed in a way that permits you to return to partial solutions.
9. Use analogies and metaphors.
10. Talk about the problem.[4]

In effective problem solving, much seems to depend on turning what is tacit knowledge into explicit information. Lochhead has designed a classroom method of problem solving for students who work in pairs to concentrate on verbalizing how they know what they know.[5] When such information becomes available to the learner, there is a better chance for recognizing common pattern systems and for triggering successful problem solutions. Where problems follow old and tested patterns, such as in mathematical and scientific learning, instruction by example is often the traditional mode and familiar algorithms suffice. But, in newer areas, such as computer studies or interdisciplinary modeling, problems may not be so identifiable, and problem solving strategies invented by the student may be the most powerful learning devices.[6]

Decison Making

Decision making might be looked upon as a subset of problem solving, but others see the ability to decide on something and live by the consequences of such choice as an entirely different kind of thinking. Decision making involves making "reasoned choices among several alternatives, choices based on judgments which are consistent with the decision maker's values."[7] The outcome of such decisions may or may not be generalizable under all conditions, because it is assumed that conditions will surely change. Decision making involves selecting the best alternatives at a particular moment in time. Such decisions are tentative and, necessarily, are based on incomplete evidence. Better decisions can be made when more is known about the topic area of discussion; the greater the certainty that can be established, the greater the chances for longer lasting decisions.

Beyer suggests a six-step method of decision making relative to the instruction of social studies:

1. Define the goal.
2. Identify obstacles to achieving the goal.
3. Identify alternatives.
4. Analyze alternatives.
5. Rank alternatives.
6. Choose the "best" alternative.[8]

It is not surprising that decision making skills are often emphasized in the social studies, areas where alternative choice making related to value dimensions is common. Fair's sequence, in which she considered how the more basic thinking skills were related to stages of coming to a decision or making a judgment, is similar (see page 28).

Adolescents, especially, are in need of practice in making wise choices, being responsible for such choices and learning to

STAGES	SKILLS IN THINKING
1. Recognizing and clarifying the decision to be made, the issues to be decided.	bringing knowledge to bear on the situation; simple analysis of the situation; raising questions
2. Proposing alternatives, two or more courses which might be chosen.	analysis in the sense of identifying key concepts, issues, value conflicts; synthesis in the sense of proposing hypothetical courses of action
3. Tracing the probable consequences of each of the alternatives.	interpreting data; analyzing data; developing requisite concepts and generalizations; application in the sense of projecting or predicting consequences for each alternative
4. Recognizing values at stake and evaluating consequences and qualifying values.	evaluation of each set of consequences; prioritizing
5. Settling upon a choice, ready to follow as the occasion requires.	evaluation as making the judgment; application[9]

live with the consequences of their decisions. Improving students' performance on essential skills and maximizing their interaction in the complex processing of decision making becomes, then, a central focus of secondary school instruction.[10]

Critical Thinking

Renewed interest in critical thinking rivals problem solving as the major focus of higher order cognitive operations in the current educational movement.[11] Like problem solving and decision making, critical thinking represents a particular approach to rational thought processing, placing emphasis on understanding meanings and on relationships between language and logic.[12]

Advocates see it as reasoned judgment, essential to fighting confusion and prejudice. The thinker's obligation to suspend judgment, wait for evidence, and carefully weigh arguments plays a major role in this higher order process.

There has been interest in critical thinking as part of the school curriculum for over 40 years. Ennis proposes general principles that have application to many subject areas:

1. A person's having a *conflict of interest* is ground for regarding that person's claim with greater suspicion than would otherwise be appropriate.
2. It is a mistake to misdescribe a person's position, and then attack the position as if it actually were the person's position (the *strawperson* fallacy).
3. Given an *if-then* statement, denial of the consequent implies the denial of the antecedent.
4. The ability of a hypothesis to *explain or help explain the facts* lends support to the hypothesis, if the hypothesis is not otherwise disqualified.[13]

Beyer extends the process of critical thinking beyond the application to language and logic and seeks to develop the dispositions as well as the operations of critical thought. He highlights ten aspects of critical thinking:

1. distinguishing between verifiable facts and value claims,
2. determining the reliability of a claim or source,
3. determining the accuracy of a statement,
4. distinguishing between warranted and unwarranted claims,
5. distinguishing relevant from irrelevant information, claims, or reasons,
6. detecting bias,
7. identifying unstated and stated assumptions,
8. identifying ambiguous or equivocal claims or arguments,
9. recognizing logical inconsistencies in a line of reasoning,
10. determining the strength of an argument.[14]

Critical thinking encourages students to challenge assumptions in order to clarify situations, then to use the logical and psychological powers they have to determine accurate judgments. For example, the affairs of everyday life differ from technical domains like mathematics, physics, and chemistry, in which concepts and assumptions are largely given.[15] In the happenings of the everyday world, assumptions need to be taken apart, clarified, and carefully reasoned by criteria that the learner understands and supports. Such thinking rightfully belongs in the school's program, and educators should be encouraged to alter the curriculum by such applications. Whether in separate courses or integrated into content areas, there are numerous ways to include critical thinking in the school's program.

While it is obvious that students do not become critical thinkers overnight, some insights on teaching critical thinking can be offered to the nation's teachers.

Use many examples of many different sorts; go slowly; be receptive to questions and to students' original thoughts; press for clarity; arrange for students to engage each other in discussion and challenge; arrange for them to assume progressively greater control over and responsibility for their learning; encourage students to be aware of what they are doing and review what they have done; ask for a focus (often a thesis) and for reasons in any discussion, and encourage students to do likewise.[16]

Critical thinking is sometimes seen as the opposite of creative thought. Some researchers see these two processes as particular ways of thinking—both significant and both required by sophisticated thinkers.

Creative Thinking

Educators have long been fascinated with exceptionally gifted persons. Current interest in creativity as a particular kind of thinking skill enables educators to examine giftedness as a potential characteristic of any youngster in a particular field or art. According to Feldman, giftedness, the realization of potential, can be achieved by any learner who selects and moves through a particular domain and achieves greater levels of sophistication by acquiring skills and understandings in it.[17] Support by teachers and parents is important, but the most critical aspect is the child's creative involvement with the domain itself. Such a position strengthens the argument for teaching thinking to all youngsters.

Eisner sees creative thinking as a major underpinning of cognitive education,[18] in that creativity enables learners to develop multiple solutions to identical problems freeing them from the *one-right-answer* syndrome. They learn to formulate questions and problems themselves and to use intuition and perception and to develop personal standards. Creative thinking strives for insight and the realization of imagination.

But, can creativity influence a thinking skills curriculum? Here again, some suggest that creativity is a particular human characteristic that ought to be developed in all youngsters because *it is different* from problem solving, decision making, and critical thinking. Creative thinking helps students develop their subjective taste and intrinsic motivation, based on aesthetic principles. Creative thinkers also exhibit mobility of thought and greater flexibility of ideas.

The cognitive level of the program design obviously reflects a rich heritage of mental processing. The overwhelming problem of school curriculum is to achieve success comprehensively. Not only must basic processes be mastered by the end of elementary school, but the roots of complex processes ought to have been planted and nurtured at the secondary level, as well.

Two other levels of thinking must still be addressed in this design—metacognition and epistemic cognition. With metacognition, the learner is enabled to become conscious of and in control of his/her learning. With epistemic thought, the learner meets the content of learning and faces the possibility of transferring thinking from one area of study to another.

METACOGNITION: The Consciousness of Thinking

The current thinking skills movement maintains that the development of *metacognition* is crucial to the development of all the cognitive processes. Ways of problem solving, anticipation of probability in decision making, awareness in critical thinking, and intuition in creativity are aspects of mental processes that can be made more tacit or real to the learner as he or she begins to study his or her own thinking. That grasp of consciousness, the cognizance of one's own actions and their effects, is the *metacognitive* component of learning, a second level of thinking.

What is metacognition to the developing student? It has been suggested that metacognition is a two-fold system that operates simultaneously as the student develops his or her cognitive abilities.[19] Figure 6 illustrates the two components of metacognitive thinking skills proposed in this design.

The monitoring of task performance is the first component and includes "study skills" frequently cited as important to school learning. The student knows what he or she must do—keep place, read directions carefully, use organizational systems (introductions, summaries, formats) to make sure the task is being approached accurately. Better student performers are keen at citing their own errors and correcting them; they pace their work carefully, especially on tests. Although these study routines seem rather mundane, they are important to develop and maintain, even in grade school. More advanced routines make the high school student a skillful learner and thinker.

The selection and understanding of strategies used in learning is the second major thrust of metacognitive activity. Studying school work is not a general process; each content area or process has a particular sequence or set of strategies that makes work in that area more efficient and significant. The student should focus on these strategies and how they relate to the content being studied. Armbruster and Anderson suggest a four-step process:

1. Focus on relevant information;
2. Relate to the material in a meaningful way, thus committing it to memory;
3. Monitor comprehension; and
4. Take corrective action when comprehension fails.[20]

In carrying out such metacognitive tasks, the student needs to know what *not* to focus on and what *not* to consider as cues and, at the same time, be aware of the importance of prior information

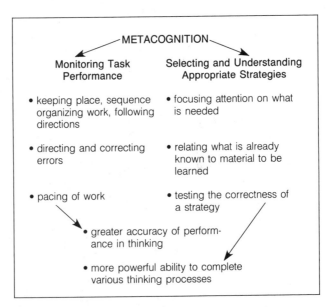

FIGURE 6. A Model of Metacognitive Thinking Skills

and knowledge. Students must seek to be risk-takers—to venture changing completely an initial approach if it appears to be a dead end. Power in metacognition means to do something efficiently and productively, not merely do more of the same. Somehow, appropriate metacognitive tasks enable the learner to get at the key concepts or the basic information needed more expeditiously. The student develops more "executive control" of his or her thinking processes as these metacognitive skills are attained.

One of the important aspects of learning that seems to appear relative to metacognition is the constructivist approach noted by Bruner and advocated by Piaget.[21] In this approach, the student becomes responsible for his or her own learning and is not dependent on the interpretation of the instructor. Self-monitoring of behavior begins with awareness of focused attention; it is also a necessary condition of being self-motivated and autonomous as a learner.[22] However, making mistakes can be fruitful. Finding the sources of one's errors is an effective way to determine that the problem or task needs to be approached differently. Such freedom to err is a first step in constructivist learning. It provides the learner with a problem to solve, a challenging mystery on which to use all the resources that the learner can uncover.

It is not surprising that the current interest in metacognition has spurred parallel interest in neuroscience and memory studies. Encoding is one of the first strategic thinking acts. There is an assumption about encoding that *the way* information is encoded determines how it is stored in the brain and, thus, how it can be retrieved. Simon speaks of how humans "chunk" the data they retain for either short- or long-term memory storage.[23] Such is the new material to be used when demanded by problem situations. Sylwester suggests that what and how the student studies can build particular patterns that create and connect concepts to be retained in the brain and, ultimately, retrieved.[24] Studies of metacognitive strategies also are beginning to address these issues, although many questions remain unanswered.

One of the most obvious strategies for enriching metacognitive learning is associated with broadening the modalities at work when studying is actually taking place. Using visual or spatial modes as well as verbal or symbolic experience can enhance learning. Feuerstein notes the importance of moving from one modality to another in his *Instrumental Enrichment* program and considers this transfer of modality part of the essence of learning certain interdependent cognitive tasks.[25] Olson considers computers as tools of the intellect, in part because they help the learner see and use information in another mode and help make tacit processes more explicit.[26] In the same vein, Salomon finds television or film intervenes effectively in a lesson because it helps the learner represent differently certain mental skills or operations.[27] He describes how a zoom lens assists the viewer in dividing complicated scenes into smaller parts and a wide angle lens actualizes the feeling of wholeness over parts.

Burns and Brooks have listed the various kinds of transformations that can help students translate thinking skills by modality shifts. Their list is challenging to a teacher who might be wrestling with the question of how to create student activities to implement such metacognitive practices. These suggestions might also raise possibilities for selecting materials within a content area that might help students understand complex concepts.

Most behaviors associated with translating can be either oral or written; and the majority are also reversible. The outline below lists the main transformations a learner could make in translating. The term "symbol" refers to any character other than a word, and the term "verbal" refers to word symbols.

I. Verbal to verbal
   A. One language to the same language
      1. Rewording—finding a synonym
      2. Converting to another form—poetry to prose
      3. Rewording—idiom to general language
      4. Rewording—simile to general language
      5. Rewording—metaphor to general language
      6. Abstracting (outlining)—lengthy to brief
      7. Abstracting—concrete to abstract
      8. Rephrasing—general language to general language
      9. Substituting—example one to example two
   B. One language to another language
      1. Rewording—finding a synonym
      2. Converting to another form—poetry to prose
      3. Rewording—idiom to general language
      4. Rewording—simile to general language
      5. Rewording—metaphor to general language
      6. Abstracting (outlining)—lengthy to brief
      7. Abstracting—concrete to abstract
II. Symbolic to verbal
   A. Symbol to word
      1. Converting—number to word

      2. Converting – abbreviations to words
      3. Converting – technical symbols to words
   B. Illustrations (two dimensional) to words
      1. Converting – drawings to words
      2. Converting – paintings to words
      3. Converting – photographs to words
      4. Converting – graphs to words
   C. Realia (three dimensional) to words
      1. Converting – objects to words
      2. Converting – object system to words
III. Symbolic to symbolic
   A. Technical symbol to technical symbol
      1. Converting – number to number
      2. Converting – letter to letter
      3. Converting – color to number
   B. Symbolic to illustration
      1. Graphing – number to drawing
IV. Symbolic to performance
   A. Illustration (two dimensional) to performance
      1. Constructing – drawing (plan) to scale model
      2. Constructing – drawing (plan) to real object
      3. Converting – music to playing
V. Verbal to performance
   A. Words or letters to performance
      1. Converting – words to hand signals
      2. Interpreting – words to actions[28]

Some metacognitive activities seek to motivate awareness of certain tacit dimensions of a problem. But, once problems are resolved and successful routines are established, good thinkers transform this fluency into unconscious states again. Sternberg notes the importance of developing an "automatic pilot" – whole strings of operations performed without conscious awareness after the learner has built up and practices specific problem resolutions over a long period of time.[29] Bloom currently is examining the development of automatic skills as related to automatic sequence.[30] Both researchers are, in fact, exploring aspects of metacognition and the development of particular learning strategies.

Metacognitive development also raises the issue of how youngsters systematically change as they intellectually mature. The sequence of ability formation seems significant to metacognition as well as to cognitive development. As the child grows in cognitive awareness, from a reliance on sensory data to conceptualizing thought in formal operations, he or she also becomes more sophisticated in metacognitive development. Adolescence, a prime time for the shift from concrete to formal thinking, seems to be an ideal period for the refinement of metacognitive tasks, especially development of strategies. Many think that the earlier the intervention of specialized experience, the more lasting the effects on learners. However, some patterns disappear at adolescence. Cohen notes that children who have "photographic" memories, who are capable of unusual retention of visual images, often lose that ability after the onset of puberty.[31]

At the heart of the current thinking skills movement is the development of metacognitive abilities parallel to cognitive operations. Everything is not known about these abilities. Indeed, questions of brain lateralization or the role of cultural influences on learning and thinking are still being researched. Nevertheless, designing a curriculum to enhance thinking ability in general cannot ignore the wealth of information about metacognition already available to the educator.

EPISTEMIC COGNITION:
The Role of Organized Knowledge

What does one think about? What role does collective knowledge, the extensive content of learned disciplines, play in the school's program? The third level of thinking in the proposed model focuses on the relationship between knowledge content and cognitive processes in the school's program and their integration for the development of thinking skills.

The first and oldest concern of schooling is that of deciding what knowledge is of most worth? Endless discussions and reports focus on what content to include or exclude from the curriculum, now and in the future. What information do students need to know? What courses do students have to study? What is basic? What is fundamental? At the elementary level, response to these questions has not changed greatly. Recent reform reports call for the same basic subjects of reading and writing, mathematics, science, and social studies that have always formed the academic core.[32] However, the addition of computer science in kindergarten through grade 12 raises a second concern: What must students *be able to do*? This is particularly an issue for college admission. What competencies do students need to be able to demonstrate so that understandings in the content areas can be generated? This would seem to be fertile ground for bringing together the world of knowledge content and the emphasis on thinking skills.

Simon points out that research on cognitive skills has taught us that expertness without extensive and accessible knowledge does not exist.[33] To be a student of history or geometry or literature, one needs to study a great deal of history, geometry, and literature. But coverage of the subject content is only part of the issue; the ways the historian, mathematician, or author thinks in his or her subject matter is yet another dimension. What issues or problems are the major concerns of a discipline? How does one work out these concerns? What problems are or are not solvable in this discipline? Over a period of time, how does the school develop concepts in the discipline and systems for adapting to new information or data in that subject context? That is the epistemic challenge of teaching thinking.

The third concern that must be considered when developing a curriculum that seeks *to be meaningful to a developing student* is, What processes are embedded in the subject content that challenge the growing intellect of the student and enhance the structure of the subject matter at the same time? Knowledge, competency, and meaningfulness are the heart of epistemic cognition in this three-level model.

It is important to remember that the state of any discipline is constantly changing. Concepts and methodologies are in a state of flux. In many academic areas today, technological developments are influencing the very nature of the discipline's progress. The major challenge to a curriculum developer is building a coherent subject area that reflects all these possible forces, yet provides a balanced view of the discipline in the classroom. This cannot be done by one teacher, nor can it happen quickly. But the need for a continuing plan of action is a requisite of curriculum planning for epistemic considerations.

Figure 7 illustrates a continuum of steps to be completed while integrating thinking skills into the curriculum. It assumes that links between the concepts of a discipline and the plan for teaching thinking in that subject matter are desirable.

The first step requires the faculty to decide what is important in their subject content and to articulate it in exact dimensions. Some disciplines may be more subject to change than others. But the greater the flux, the greater the need for this conversation. Step 2 requires teachers to consider the various thinking skills and the ways they are embedded in the disciplines. It is hoped that the sequence of skill development may emerge during discussion at this stage of the continuum; but, by the third step, the continuum calls for articulating this very progression. Staff may find that some subject areas have been organized erroneously, such as generalizing before careful comparisons are made. If this is the

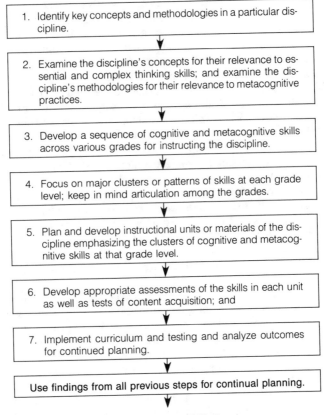

1. Identify key concepts and methodologies in a particular discipline.

2. Examine the discipline's concepts for their relevance to essential and complex thinking skills; and examine the discipline's methodologies for their relevance to metacognitive practices.

3. Develop a sequence of cognitive and metacognitive skills across various grades for instructing the discipline.

4. Focus on major clusters or patterns of skills at each grade level; keep in mind articulation among the grades.

5. Plan and develop instructional units or materials of the discipline emphasizing the clusters of cognitive and metacognitive skills at that grade level.

6. Develop appropriate assessments of the skills in each unit as well as tests of content acquisition; and

7. Implement curriculum and testing and analyze outcomes for continued planning.

Use findings from all previous steps for continual planning.

FIGURE 7. Integrating Thinking Skills into a
Subject Curriculum

case, the sequence can be corrected at this step. Step 4 involves a selection; everything cannot be taught or included in the curriculum. Select the most powerful skills at a grade level and focus students' work on them. Balance and adequate representation is important, and so is articulation among several grades. Step 5 is the heart of the development process. It may be possible to find ready-made materials for this step, but at least the prior steps will have prepared staff to know which materials they need. Step 6 assumes some kind of assessment and reminds the practitioner that instruments should be reflective of the curriculum's cognitive design, as well as be related to the particular subject content. By Step 7, outcomes from assessment should be apparent and should be used for further planning. The overall design becomes a series of corrected approximations.

There is a growing body of literature in various disciplines that indicates scholars in the field have already begun to work on various steps of a suggested thinking continuum. Language arts specialists are examining the teaching of reading with respect to its cognitive and metacognitive dimensions.[34] Major program efforts already exist in grade-relevant curricula for teaching reading in terms of cognitive strategies.[35] Similarly, attention is also being focused on written communication in terms of its relevance to the development of higher order skills, particularly critical thinking.[36] Mathematics both at elementary and secondary levels are directing curricular concerns to how students process information and how they work at mathematical problems.[37] In various areas of natural science, the relevance of problem solving is seriously being debated.[38] Decision making and critical thinking are focuses of several examinations of the social studies.[39] There is a paucity of literature on the interrelationships of different disciplines across the instructional program, but that is definitely a long-term goal of the thinking skills movement. Billington suggests that "in the third century of our nation's history, the most pressing problem in higher education is to integrate the ancient traditions of the liberal arts with the modern imperatives of our technological society."[40] In a sense, that is the essence of the school's epistemic problem—to teach the knowledge accumulated in the disciplines of the past in terms of the skills required for 21st century thinking. By approaching collections of information in terms of essential and complex thinking, as well as relating them to metacognitive processing, we are beginning to wrestle with that dilemma, but elementary and secondary educators will have to join forces with theoreticians in higher education to resolve it. The elusive, ideal curriculum need not be a figment of an educational planner's imagination. It can become an instructional reality, if we are seriously committed to building it cooperatively.

QUESTIONS ABOUT THE THREE-LEVEL MODEL

The three-level model of thinking is not an exact prescription for a curriculum for teaching thinking. It suggests questions that ought to be answered in developing such a curriculum and indicates limits within which those responses might be made. Much must be left to actual implementation to resolve. What models of instruction are appropriate? Should instruction be content-free or content-based? If so, when? How should testing be organized? These issues will be examined in Chapter 3.

Finally, the question can be asked, What sequence of courses best presents thinking skills to the student? Again, there is no singular curriculum that can guarantee the teaching of thinking. Much depends on what happens in the individual classroom. But the program design developed in this study suggests some guidelines for developing a K-12 scope and sequence based on the nature of the essential and complex skills and their relationship to metacognitive and epistemic cognition.

These guidelines include:

- Initial emphasis in the primary grades (K-4) should be on the essential processes of qualification, classification, and relationships. To the extent that students can work at transformation or causation, those processes can also be introduced.
- Middle grades (5-8) students should continue to work on qualification, classification, and relationships but emphasis should be placed on the development of transformation and causation processes. To the extent that students can work on complex processes of problem solving, decision making, critical thinking, and creative thinking, those processes can be introduced.
- Upper grades (9-12) students should continue to work on essential processes but emphasis should be placed on the development of complex processes and the special relationship of these processes in particular course work, that is, in specific disciplines and the problems and concepts of these disciplines.
- Metacognitive development should be stressed in all grades with an early emphasis at the primary level on task monitoring activity or study skills. Strategy development can parallel the introduction of the essential processes of transformation and causation and work in the four complex processes, mainly during late middle school or junior high grades. Strategies should be related to the conceptual requirements of particular subject areas as well.
- Specific courses required in the curriculum should represent various epistemological bases and opportunities for modality development. Course work should also be selected so that students in the upper grades have the opportunity to work in all the complex processes with in-depth discipline experience.

When considering the content dimensions of the curriculum, the influence of various modalities should also be kept in mind. Courses like English, reading, social studies and civics, and foreign language are verbal in emphasis. Mathematics is quantitative and has applications in chemistry and certain aesthetic activities that stress measurement or tempo. Subjects such as geometry, drafting, the graphic arts, and computer science emphasize spatial learning. Students need to study in all the modalities, and a full curriculum should include academic variety in a rich mixture. The several thinking skills can then be developed in depth in the various contents, and subject interrelationships can be sought.

---

1. Karen S. Kitchener, "Cognition, Metacognition, and Epistemic Cognition: A Three-Level Model of Cognitive Processing," *Human Development* 26 (1983): 222-232; Barbara Z. Presseisen, "Thinking Skills: Meanings and Models," in *Developing Minds: A Resource Book for Teaching Thinking*, Arthur L. Costa, ed. (Alexandria, VA: Association for Supervision and Curriculum Development, 1985), 43-48.

2. Robert Karplus, *Science Curriculum Improvement Study: Relative Position and Motion* (Chicago: Rand McNally, 1967).

3. Herbert A. Simon, "Problem Solving and Education," in *Problem Solving and Education: Issues in Teaching and Research*, David T. Tuma and Frederick Reif, eds. (Hillsdale, NJ: Lawrence Erlbaum Associates, 1980), 81-96.

4. Moshe E. Rubinstein, *Patterns of Problem Solving* (Englewood Cliffs, NJ: Prentice-Hall, 1975).

5. Jack Lochhead, "Research Synthesis on Problem Solving," *Educational Leadership* 39 (1981): 68-70.

6. Simon, "Problem Solving and Education."

7. Edward W. Cassidy and Dana G. Kurfman, "Decision Making as Purpose and Promise," in *Developing Decision-Making Skills*, 47th Year Book, Dana G. Kurfman, ed. (Washington, D.C.: National Council for the Social Studies, 1977): 1-26.

8. Barry K. Beyer, "What's in a Skill? Defining the Thinking Skills We Teach," *Social Science Record* 21 (1984): 19.

9. Jean Fair, "Skills in Thinking," in *Developing Decision-Making Skills*, 47th Year Book, Dana G. Kurfman, ed. (Washington, D.C.: National Council for the Social Studies, 1977): 29-68.

10. Herbert J. Klausmeier, James M. Lipham, and John C. Daresh, *The Renewal and Improvement of Secondary Education: Concepts and Practices* (New York: University Press of America, 1983).

11. Barbara Z. Presseisen, *Critical Thinking and Thinking Skills: State of the Art Definitions and Practice in Public Schools* (Philadelphia, PA: Research for Better Schools, Inc., 1986).

12. Richard W. Paul, "The Critical-Thinking Movement," *National Forum* 65 (1985): 2-3.

13. Robert H. Ennis, "Critical Thinking and the Curriculum," *National Forum* 65 (1985): 28-31.

14. Barry K. Beyer, "What's in a Skill?," p. 20.

15. Richard W. Paul, "Critical Thinking: Fundamental to Education for a Free Society," *Educational Leadership* 42 (1984): 4-14.

16. Robert H. Ennis, "Critical Thinking and the Curriculum," p. 30.

17. David H. Feldman, "Piaget on Giftedness—A Very Short Essay," *The Genetic Epistemologist* 12 (1983): 1-10; David H. Feldman, "The Child as Craftsman," *Thinking* 6 (1985): 20-24.

18. Elliot W. Eisner, "Creative Education in American Schools Today," *educational HORIZONS* 63 (Special Edition, 1985): 10-15.

19. John H. Flavell, "Metacognitive Aspects of Problem Solving," in *The Nature of Intelligence*, Lauren B. Resnick, ed. (Hillsdale, NJ: Lawrence Erlbaum Associates, 1976).

20. Bonnie B. Armbruster and Thomas H. Anderson, "Research Synthesis on Study Skills," *Educational Leadership* 39 (1981): 156.

21. Jerome Bruner, "Models of the Learner," *Educational Researcher* 14 (1985): 5-8.

22. Constance Kamii, "Autonomy: The Aim of Education Envisioned by Piaget," *Phi Delta KAPPAN* 65 (1984): 410-415.

23. Herbert A. Simon, "Problem Solving and Education."

24. Robert Sylwester, "Research on Memory: Major Discoveries and Major Educational Challenges," *Educational Leadership* 42 (1985): 69-75.

25. Reuven Feuerstein et al., "Instrumental Enrichment and Intervention Program for Structural Cognitive Modifiability: Theory and Practice," in *Thinking and Learning Skills*, vol. 1, Judith W. Segal, Susan F. Chipman, and Robert Glaser, eds. (Hillsdale, NJ: Lawrence Erlbaum Associates, 1985), 43-82.

26. David R. Olson, "Computers as Tools of the Intellect," *Educational Researcher* 14 (1985): 5-7.

27. Gavriel Salomon, *Interaction of Media, Cognition, and Learning* (San Francisco: Jossey-Bass, 1979).

28. Richard W. Burns and Gary D. Brooks, "Processes, Problem Solving, and Curriculum Reform," *Educational Technology* 10 (1970): 10.

29. Robert J. Sternberg, "The Nature of Mental Abilities," *American Psychologist* 34 (1979): 214-230.

30. Benjamin Bloom, "Automaticity," *Educational Leadership* 43 (1986): 70-77.

31. Jozef Cohen, *Thinking* (Chicago: Rand McNally, 1971).

32. Barbara Z. Presseisen, *Unlearned Lessons: Current and Past Reforms for School Improvement* (Philadelphia and London: Falmer Press, 1985).

33. Herbert A. Simon, "Problem Solving and Education."

34. Ann L. Brown, *Teaching Students to Think as They Read: Implications for Curriculum Reform* (Paper prepared for the American Educational Research Association Project: Research Contributions for Educational Improvement, 1985); Jeanne S. Chall, *Stages of Reading Development* (New York: McGraw-Hill, 1983).

35. Beau F. Jones, Minda R. Amiran, and Michael Katims, "Teaching Cognitive Strategies and Text Structures Within Language Arts Programs," in *Learning and Thinking Skills*, Judith W. Segal, Susan F. Chipman, and Robert Glaser, eds. (Hillsdale, NJ: Lawrence Erlbaum Associates, 1985).

36. Carol B. Olson, "Fostering Critical Thinking Skills Through Writing," *Educational Leadership* 42 (1984): 28-39; Marlene Scardamalia, "Higher Order Abilities: Written Communication" (Paper presented for the American Educational Research Association Project: Research Contributions for Educational Improvement, 1984).

37. Alan H. Schoenfeld, "Psychology and the Mathematical Method," *Education and Urban Society* 17 (1985): 387-403.

38. Jill H. Larkin, "Teaching Problem Solving in Physics: The Psychological Laboratory and the Practical Classroom," in *Problem Solving and Education: Issues in Teaching and Research*, David T. Tuma and Frederick Reif, eds. (Hillsdale, NJ: Lawrence Erlbaum Associates, 1980).

39. Barry K. Beyer, "Critical Thinking Revisited," *Social Education* 49 (1985): 268-302.

40. David P. Billington, "Engineering and the Liberal Arts" (An address at the presidential inauguration of Drexel University, 27 April 1985, Philadelphia, PA, 1985).

3

IMPLEMENTATION

Having a program design for teaching thinking skills is the first step in improving students' cognitive performance. Implementing that design requires the involvement and commitment of the school's professional staff. Key areas that need to be examined are classroom instruction, assessment, materials development, ongoing staff development, and relating thinking skills beyond the school's program.

CLASSROOM INSTRUCTION

Whether the teaching of thinking skills should be by direct or indirect instruction is highly controversial. Most researchers advocate the direct instruction of thinking in the classroom and stress the importance of metacognitive understanding of the processes involved.[1] This is not to say that intuitive or indirect learning is not valuable or effective; many thinking skill advocates would probably praise discovery learning. But the current theorists are *functionally* oriented; they see these indirect approaches as inefficient and time consuming, in light of the extensive list of thinking skills that need to be mastered. Some researchers contend that indirect experience alone may not be sufficient for students to master the thinking task.[2]

Beyer has developed an instructional sequence for direct instruction that includes the following strategies:

1. Introduce the skill.
2. Explain the skill.
3. Demonstrate the skill.
4. Apply the skill.
5. Reflect on the skill.[3]

How might this skill sequence be applied to the processes presented in the program design? The following lesson on analysis is based on Beyer's sequence. It utilizes the steps of direct instruction in combination with selected materials. The purpose is to engage the learner in an experience designed to introduce the skill and to provide practice in using the skill on additional problems that require concrete analytical thinking. This particular lesson, based on Robert Leighton's "Gone but Not Forgotten" page in *Games Magazine*, can be used with adults or children.

DIRECT TEACHING LESSON EXAMPLE
SKILL: ANALYSIS

1. Introduce the Skill

Define: Separation of whole into component parts.

Examination of the relationship of parts to how something operates.

Emphasis on utility: the missing segment or part makes an object impossible to work; the segment or part is key to making the object useful.

2. Explain the Skill

In this lesson, there are several objects to be analyzed for their missing parts. They are all common, real-life objects that could be used by anyone.

What is missing in each object is directly related to the usefulness of that object.

It may be useful to scan the various objects when you start to find one that you understand easily. Then go back and compare that object to the resolution of the other objects.

Try to develop a rule for your operation or solving of the task.

3. Demonstrate the Skill

Use an overhead transparency to show the initial example of an object to be analyzed. The same object will appear on the task sheet.

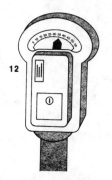

1. What is the object?
2. What does it do? How do you use it?
3. Tell the sequence of the steps you would perform in using it.
4. Determine what is missing in this object? (Have you formed a rule?)
5. Explain how this deficiency makes the object useless. (This is an application of the rule.)
6. Note the difficulties you might have (even temporarily) in analyzing this particular object.

Sample object to be analyzed.

4. Students Apply the Skill

Pass out the handout page; let the students work on the tasks – alone or with partners. Observe the skill being applied.

GONE BUT NOT FORGOTTEN   by Robert Leighton

Each of the twelve items on this page is missing one important element that makes it very difficult, if not impossible, to use. Can you get a handle on just what's missing here?

From "Gone but Not Forgotten," p. 40, by Robert Leighton, Games Magazine *9 (1985), reprinted by permission of* Games Magazine.

5. Reflect on the Skill

Were there compounding difficulties? What were they? Did prior knowledge seem important on any or all the objects?

What other classroom applications use "analysis"? How do they differ from this example?

Can you develop other examples of classroom work that use analysis? How are they like or not like this example?

What have you learned about your own ways of thinking? Could you improve on your thinking?

It is interesting to note that when this lesson is used with adults, they, like children, are driven to seek the correct answers. They are not especially attuned to studying their own strategies and responses. This is a concrete learning experience, and it is also culturally relevant. For instance, the objects familiar to adults may not be familiar to inner city children. Still, there are symbolic or linguistic learnings to be made almost incidentally from the discussion of the correct answers. The lacing between the thumb and forefinger on a baseball mitt is called "webbing." The rope that raises or lowers a flag is called the "halyard." This lesson is not designed to apply thinking skills to a particular content area. That is another topic, which some say should be raised only *after* the direct instruction of the skill itself has occurred.

The question of whether or not thinking skills should be content-based is another issue that has been discussed; and, at first glance, there appears to be little agreement among experts on this question. Feuerstein and his colleagues have built a curriculum noticeably devoid of content, unfettered by the nuances of subject matter.[4] Both Simon and Glaser, on the other hand, maintain that real command of thinking processes is only embedded in various contents of schooling.[5] The learner ultimately must think about something. The expert performer knows intimately how the information of the discipline interrelates with the special ways of processing that data. The better thinker, says Sternberg, is more able to figure out how a problem is constructed, and, once he or she has determined that relationship, is quicker and more accurate in working through to the solution.[6]

There is really more agreement here than first meets the eye. Feuerstein and colleagues are addressing the *instructional* question, the pedagogical problem of how to help students overcome learning deficits. Both Simon and Glaser speak in *formative* terms, by describing what ought to be on the basis of what has proven to be the past successful sequence of an expert performer. They set an epistemological goal that strives for the best of thinking in

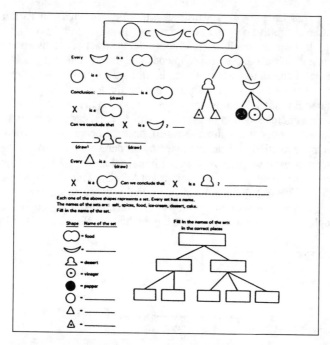

FIGURE 8. Instrumental Enrichment Task on
Forming Hierarchies

*From Instrumental Enrichment, an intervention program for struc-
tural cognitive modifiability by R. Feuerstein et al, (p. 73). In J.
W. Segal, S. F. Chipman & R. Glaser, (Eds.) Thinking and learning skills, 1985, Hillsdale, NJ: Lawrence Erlbaum. Reprinted by
permission.*

a subject area. Perhaps this is what higher education should strive
for. But it is necessary that that goal be seen through the eyes and
minds of the novice students at the elementary and secondary levels. Obviously, it is appropriate for a student's initial experience
in working with a particular process to identify it, to see how it
works, and to learn when and by what rules it operates. Once this
is achieved separately from content, learning to use that skill in
particular content areas will enrich the student's understanding of
the skill and help the learner discover the nuances of relationships
that make the skill operable in more complex ways.

Figure 8 is an example of how students learn about hierarchical classification. They study the symbolic attributes and learn to
relate certain kinds of objects in particular ways. The puzzle-like
quality of organizing information is highlighted.

This task involves working with rules drawn from earlier learned cognitive processes based in classification and relationships. The learner experiences developing the abstract relationships of sets and subsets and learns to encode and decode using signs. Although Feuerstein sees this lesson in forming syllogisms as content-free, the success of the task depends on the learner's knowledge of certain foods. What is important is that even though the content is not yet embedded in the subject matter of an academic curriculum (unless one is in culinary school), once the operation is learned, it can be applied to understanding any academic content. After the students have worked through the initial thinking process and are ready for content, then it is important to relate that content to the kinds of thinking the student is gradually going to master.

School curriculum should document the growing cognitive sophistication of the learner and the gradual development of think-

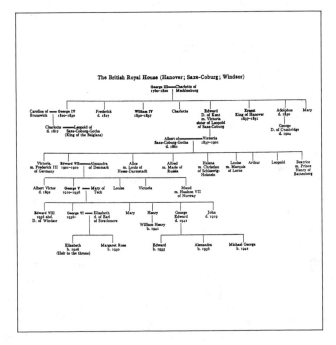

FIGURE 9. The British Royal House as a Basis
For Hierarchical Applications

From An Encyclopedia of World History, *by William L. Langer. Copyright 1940, 1948, 1952, and © 1968, 1972 by Houghton Mifflin Company. Reprinted by permission of Houghton Mifflin Company.*

ing in several parallel subject matters. Adolescents, in studying the genealogy of the British royal house, for example, could trace relationships among European nations before either World War I or II or raise questions about the health of the tsarevich of Russia, given what is known about the transmission of hemophilia through the family bloodline (see Figure 9).

In terms of instruction, then, there is no conflict between content and process in the thinking skills curriculum. Current researchers suggest that it is important for the student to be able to complete the necessary cognitive tasks consistent with their level of sophistication in any given discipline. They advise that, initially, students should learn the particular aspects of the thinking skill without the distraction of subject content, followed by gradual application to appropriate subject matters.

Educators should not assume that this instructional sequence is linear or directional. As Piaget often reiterates, the learner must frequently go back and forth between prior understanding and a new depiction, studying the differences in more and more instances until, finally, the latter form dominates. Beyer's direct instructional model calls for providing additional examples, after the first instance is learned, and suggests that teachers introduce alternative media as the student becomes more proficient in the skill. Eventually, in teaching the complex processes, subject matter in depth must be included in the curriculum so that the student can wrangle with problems similar to or in anticipation of those of the full-fledged historian or scientist. The essential instructional challenge, however, is to balance the teaching of a particular thinking skill with appropriate content in ways consistent with the learner's developmental knowledge level and prior cognitive experience.

The instruction of thinking skills can benefit from recent findings associated with effective schools research and application. The importance of high expectations on the teacher's part is one of the variables often cited in this research.[7] The heart of the constructivist approach to instruction is the teacher's belief that all students can learn the various thinking processes involved in the curriculum and expect them to do so. To this end, they design lessons so that students can monitor themselves, they organize individual and group responsibility so that the students can work through difficulty and error, and they present information and materials in various formats for different learning styles and more personalized meaning.

Requiring the active participation of every student is another aspect of effective schools research. Brown suggests that computers can be useful as tools of learning in such an active environment; he stresses that the user-friendly quality of microcomputers enhances the positive learning climate of a successful classroom.[8] Finally, it is important to design instruction as a cooperative venture between students and teacher, and as a collaborative enterprise among teachers and administrators. The more the active participants discuss and understand the objectives of instruction, the greater the likelihood for both ownership and effectiveness.

ASSESSMENT

The current thinking skills movement places more emphasis on assessing student progress than on merely checking it by examination. The emphasis is on diagnostic assessment, finding out how the student is doing, what the student is thinking, and, most important, why. The implication is that useful information should be gathered about student performance so that teaching can be fine-tuned for the individual student's benefit. This approach reflects the findings of effective schools research, and, more appropriately, meets the needs of metacognitive instruction, an immediate concern of the functional teaching of thinking. What does this mean to the classroom geared for the effective teaching of thinking?

Thinking skills need to be assessed in various ways, especially as associated with performance. Many published tests have been criticized for doing a poor job of checking performance.[9] Sternberg points out that very few standardized tests assess more than content, rarely asking students to consider what complex processes are involved in a test item.[10] Pencil and paper instruments of short answer variety are convenient measures for mass examination, but uniform scoring practices associated with them often obliterate opportunities for really finding out what students think and why. Careful questioning sequences may be as useful a diagnostic device as an instructional tool, but they require face-to-face contact between the teacher and the student. Testing, Feuerstein would surely concur, is part of the mediation of learning.

It might be said that in the thinking skills curriculum, criterion-referenced testing is more promising than norm-referenced testing.[11] Criterion-referenced testing, directed toward what the student knows about the content and what he or she can do with the content, is much more appropriate for encouraging the student to work independently. If 30% or 40% of the student population falls below accepted levels of performance, the assessment question is, Why does this happen on academic tests? In what ways can instruction be altered to help students make the mental connections required by the test? That is the essence of a classroom climate conducive to learning. As Piaget has said, the problem is not "Why did the student miss the question and create error?" but, "What question did the student answer?"[12] The assessment concern is not one of minimum competency but of maximum productivity. How can we find out how well the student thinks or how fertile his or her abilities are in terms of developing higher order reasoning? Bracey notes the confusion between *minimum competency* and the *basics*.[13] In the proposed program design, the essential thinking skills are basic to the student's ability to progress toward the mastery of higher order, more complex processes. Evaluating that development lies at the heart of assessment in teaching thinking and should reflect both cognitive and metacognitive performance. Competent teachers are cognizant of the potential patterns of error in their subject area and knowledgeable about different ways to remediate insufficient learning.

The current thinking skills movement has implications for assessment in the classroom relative to a student's potential success. Tests should be geared to each student's level of thinking complexity. Items should be appropriate for cognitive as well as content objectives. Teachers might want to consider more than one measure of a particular skill and test in varied modalities. They should observe *how* students work through a problem. The background knowledge required to answer a question should be carefully weighed. Tests need not be solely idiosyncratic devices; sometimes group examinations can teach more and enable students to learn from their peers. Teachers should consider the relationships between classroom or departmental testing and standardized examinations used by a district's central office. Finally, grading should be designed to capture the greatest potential for student progress, not serve as a sorting system of ascertained failure.

SELECTION OF APPROPRIATE MATERIALS

Selecting or developing appropriate instructional materials is a third aspect of classroom implementation that must be addressed when planning for teaching thinking. The concerns for learning noted in Figure 1 (p. 6) of the instructional design pertain to planning these actual instructional events; none is more important than the best materials to inspire and guide the student's action. Curriculum guides advertise what is being taught in school, and they usually include the goals and expectations of learning, the list of specific subject matter to be covered, and suggested or available instructional resources. Beyer calls for some other specific additions to a curriculum guide that seeks to include thinking among its objectives:

- explication of the thinking processes which are part of the lesson or unit,
- the developmental sequence of the particular thinking skills across the grades or subject area,
- careful definitions of these skills and appropriate procedures to teach them, and
- rules associated with the skills' most effective application.[14]

He believes that decisions concerning these curricular tasks must be made *before* materials can be sought or lessons designed. This model of teacher competency is clearly in opposition to the notion of "teacher-proof" materials advocated in the 1960s. The current thinking skills movement seeks the professional autonomy of the teacher as much as it strives for the student's growing independence in learning.[15]

What are appropriate instructional materials for teaching thinking? The potential is enormous. Pratt provides an excellent list of over a hundred kinds of resources to be translated into classroom activities (see Figure 10 in Chapter 4). In the teaching of thinking, the significance of sound selection seems crucial. Hunkins refers to Scheffler's list of six criteria of materials selection which can be applied by staff leaders working on thinking:

- Economy—Does the learner attain maximum self-sufficiency in the most economical manner by using these materials?
- Significance—Do these materials contribute to the main emphases of teaching thinking, and to the targeted skill(s) in particular?
- Validity—How authentic is the content of the materials selected and how congruent are these materials in light of the objectives of this lesson/unit?
- Interest—How likely is it that these materials will capture the interest of the students and cater to or foster their participatory activity?
- Learnability—Are these materials appropriate for the particular students who are to experience the curriculum?
- Feasibility—Can the materials be used in the time allowed, with the current funding resources, and by the available staff?[16]

Over time, a body of materials can be located and original materials can be generated that provide a viable base for thinking skills instruction. But this is not a task to be completed overnight or in one or two weeks. Finding such material is a challenge to the instructional staff, and it can be enjoyable and constructive. What is essential is that teachers take note of the effects of the materials as students use them. Teacher-made materials can be useful, but often the best match of materials to student needs can be made by re-ordering and adapting purchased items. Ideally, instructional and assessment materials should be coordinated. A recent publication of the Center for Performance Assessment suggests that teachers keep track of test items and build a file bank of good items to amass useful assessment materials for teaching higher cognitive skills.[17]

The emphasis on selecting sound materials for thinking skills instruction does not preclude buying a published program. Numerous programs already exist, and the materials, as well as staff training packages included with them, are available to schools across the country. The program design presented here calls for a curriculum package that would serve an entire design. Some programs address only the essential skills or perhaps focus on only one of the complex skills. It is important that potential consumers know what their school population needs, what a particular program offers, how well it provides for or meets all their objectives, and whether the cost of such a program is appropriate for their school or district's resources. Then decisions can be made to build the best possible materials base for their students.

Chapter 4 contains exemplary materials that might be employed to serve the requirements of a comprehensive thinking skills program. Appendix A is a sample teacher checklist/evaluation form for selecting materials for a thinking skills program. Educators are encouraged to use this checklist and to adapt it for their own purposes.

ONGOING STAFF DEVELOPMENT

The fate of most improvement practices rests in the hands of those who implement them—teachers and administrators at the school level. Thus, the most critical challenge to developing a good thinking skills program is the preparation of staff who will implement it. Research has shown that changes are more enduring when they are not imposed from the top nor generated solely by the work force itself.[18] An important tenet of the current thinking skills movement is that building a sound thinking skills program within the curriculum requires collaborative planning and dialogue among participants at all levels of the school system. Ongoing staff development, inservice, and staff committee responsibilities make this collaboration real in the life of the teaching staff. Moreover, such mechanisms are the basis for developing particular structures that lead thinking skills instruction.

Staff development is not a "quick-fix," nor is it entertainment.

Staff development activities should be well planned and lead to actions or decisions that will be implemented and evaluated. Such activities ought to depend on school leaders' awareness of research literature and policy formation. Ideally, a core committee of interested school staff will emerge to lead the school's program. In large districts, research personnel may be available to serve as liaisons and spokespersons. Support from the superintendent's office, the curriculum staff, and union or professional association leadership is important to a successful and united effort.

What might a staff development program to support thinking skills instruction look like? Dorr-Bremme emphasizes that programs planned jointly should strive to meet four criteria. Practices:

1. should be proximal to the everyday instructional tasks teachers need to accomplish: planning their teaching, diagnosing students' learning needs, monitoring their progress through the curriculum-as-taught, placing students in appropriate groupings and instructional programs, adjusting their teaching in light of students' progress, and informing parents and others about how students are doing
2. should be consonant, from teachers' perspectives, with the curriculum that teachers are actually teaching
3. should be immediately accessible to teachers, so that teachers can give them to students when the time seems appropriate and have results available promptly
4. should be designed to include a variety of performance "contexts," i.e., different types of response formats and tasks.[19]

In the beginning, a program of staff development should be designed for each school or district in which teachers are integral. Lieberman stresses that "teacher-to-teacher links" are an essential part of building teacher ownership of a program.[20] This is a prerequisite for program success. Involvement develops an important constituency, and, as teachers participate in the planning of the program, they become more involved in the decision making process. Purkey and Degen see involvement as a basis for ownership; but even more important, they interpret it as the "most effective way to generate a sense of commitment to the innovative process and [to] create the necessary flexibility to address local conditions and needs."[21]

In dealing with the issue of program design, key questions about how the staff envisions thinking will come to the fore:

• What is meant by thinking processes or skills?
• Are these processes and skills already accounted for or addressed in the existing program?

- What scope and sequence supports it?
- What deficits do our students have in essential or complex processes?
- How adequate is our current curriculum guide for meeting our thinking skills needs?

It is imperative that the instructional staff talk to one another about these questions, not just once or twice a year but on a continuing basis. They need to consider their own responses and, in some cases, they may need to gather data or survey their own members to resolve issues. A faculty's answers to the questions will shape the staff development program in which they will participate. They will also recast the curriculum guide that documents the school or district's intent to the larger school community.

Inservice programs regularly address several topics that also need to be part of effective staff development for teaching thinking. Instructional techniques and strategies, sharing materials, and testing and grading practices always interest classroom instructors, but thinking skill instruction raises additional issues that can be pursued through staff development:

- What questioning techniques enhance classroom learning?
- How can grouping and assignments in class be made more effective?
- How do thinking skills apply to my particular discipline?
- How can we make better use of available test data?
- How can teachers work more cooperatively to improve classroom effectiveness?

A thinking skills program will build credibility if it proceeds to answer such questions in a nonthreatening way and emphasizes that such change is valued. Resources or even outside expertise may be needed to deal with these issues adequately, depending on the services and materials available at a particular site.

One of the great dangers of any curriculum development task is the possibility that the new practice can become a frill. To avoid this, it is important that staff development programs address both compliance and evaluation. If a school system is serious about the development of thinking skills instruction, then it must expect honest responses from faculty and their sincere desire to change. It seeks to find out what happens in the classroom when the program is implemented, and, most important, the system provides services and materials along the way to facilitate change. This would seem to require staff development programs to help teachers deal with three important aspects of curriculum development:

- developing an exemplary or generic lesson plan to show teachers how thinking might be instituted in a classroom;
- determining a general teacher algorithm, a model of good teaching that can be used for self-monitoring; and
- elucidation of questions that might be posed to the students themselves so that areas for change in particular classrooms and in the curriculum can be earmarked.

It should be emphasized that the reason for developing these materials is to assist staff in doing their tasks more effectively. Used punitively, such materials could not only destroy the collegial atmosphere that is desired among staff, but undermine the spirit of trust that binds the very ethos of the school. Appendices B, C, and D include exemplary materials for staff development concerns related to the tasks noted.

Finally, staff development programs should not ignore the impact of materials and past practice on educators. Selecting appropriate materials requires knowing what is needed for a particular school population and what actually constitutes practical success. Publisher displays at national meetings attest to American teachers' attraction to new educational products. Sharing curriculum guides and communicating among schools regarding the teaching of thinking skills should also be encouraged.

RELATING THINKING SKILLS BEYOND THE SCHOOL'S PROGRAM

The last concern of implementation in advancing thinking skills has to do with relating thinking and its instruction beyond the school's program. At least two major concerns are emphasized: first is the necessity to create alliances between school practitioners and professional improvement efforts to support better instruction. The second thrust is to connect thinking with the real world and the activities that go on there.

Thinking is not the preserve of only elementary and secondary education. Obviously, it is a central focus in the university world and to the many disciplines that make their home in academe. Common subject matter and its instruction should be a mutual concern of American teachers and professors. Unfortunately, the most cordial relations among these instructors do not exist. But cooperation, at least with regard to the nature of subject content and concerns of teaching it, must be sought if thinking skills are really to be understood and pursued at higher order levels in schools and colleges. The rejuvenation of teacher education could be built on such an agenda, and interdisciplinary understandings across the curriculum might well be explored at the same time.[22] The whole concept of the classroom or the school utilized as a "laboratory," in Dewey's sense of the word, can be applied best in the teaching of and about thinking. Specifically, the professors of future teachers should examine the direct instruction of thinking and gauge its success or failings. California Superintendent of Instruction Honig calls for these professors to provide the intellectual leadership necessary for "designing curricula for a variety of children."[23] Because California's majority population soon will consist of minorities, it is easy to understand Honig's concern. It is appropriate, then, that California develops an extensive thinking skills program.[24]

Educators who are interested in teaching thinking have other professional associations to work with beyond universities and teacher training institutions. Organizations like the American Educational Research Association, the Association for Supervision and Curriculum Development, the National Council for the Social Studies, the National Council of Teachers of Mathematics, the American Association of School Administrators, the National Association of Secondary School Principals, and the National Council of Teachers of English all have begun to address the teaching of thinking. Teachers should examine materials produced by these groups, consider the training programs and seminars they offer, attend meetings and conferences held regionally and nationally. The American Federation of Teachers and the National Education Association also have begun to work in the areas of critical thinking skills. All these efforts are potential resources for classroom instructors who seek the best materials and the most useful advice about how to organize a thinking skills program. There is no "one way" to teach thinking; the dialogue and the exchange cannot help but enrich a school's program and every teacher's expertise.

It is important to connect a school's thinking skills program with the real world of work and society beyond the school. Thinking is not merely a concern of the college bound; all students need to be cognizant of the abilities, the competencies, and the strategies that are required by a particular job or a special interest. No area seems more relevant to this than the need to find one's way in the sophisticated technology of the emerging industrial scene. The recent reform report of the National Science Board speaks to the "new basics" of the 21st century:

> We must return to basics, but the "basics" of the 21st century are not only reading writing and arithmetic. They include

communication and higher problem-solving skills, and scientific and technological literacy—the *thinking* tools that allow us to understand the technological world around us.[25]

Besides emphasizing the need to address these skills as early as elementary school and continuing to develop them through high school, the Commission's report emphasizes that youngsters need a healthy exposure to the kinds of thinking that real workers do when they are on the job. Students need to become aware that higher level performance and good study skills are not only the concerns of the classroom teacher and the college bound. They are critical to an employer's interest, the basis of a worker's compensation, and result in lifelong deficits if they are not developed early in one's academic career. Teachers need to build links between the community and the classroom to place thinking skills instruction in the context of the real world.

Implementation, then, requires that educators be alert to ways of relating the thinking skills program to the students' world and to the abilities required to master its tools and technologies, including the world of the computer, in order to operate intelligently in society itself. With a program design in mind and with the essentials of implementation in place, the task that emerges as the practitioner's real challenge is that of finding resources upon which to build both the teachers' and the students' activities for instruction. This is the focus of the next chapter.

1. Barry K. Beyer, "Critical Thinking Revisited," *Social Education* 49 (1985): 268-302; Reuven Feuerstein et al., "Instrumental Enrichment, an Intervention Program for Structural Cognitive Modifiability: Theory and Practice," in *Thinking and Learning Skills*, vol. 1, Judith W. Segal, Susan F. Chipman, and Robert Glaser, eds. (Hillsdale, NJ: Lawrence Erlbaum Associates, 1985), 43-82; Raymond S. Nickerson, "Thoughts on Teaching Thinking," *Educational Leadership* 39 (1981): 21-24.

2. Catherine Cornbleth, "Critical Thinking and Cognitive Process," in *Review of Research in Social Studies Education 1976-1983*, Bulletin 75, William B. Stanley et al., eds. (Boulder, CO: ERIC Clearinghouse for Social Studies/Social Science Education, 1985), 11-63.

3. Barry K. Beyer, "Common Sense About Teaching Thinking Skills," *Educational Leadership* 41 (1983): 46.

4. Reuven Feuerstein et al., "Instrumental Enrichment, an Intervention Program for Structural Cognitive Modifiability: Theory and Practice," in *Thinking and Learning Skills*, vol. 1, Judith W. Segal, Susan F. Chipman, and Robert Glaser, eds. (Hillsdale, NJ: Lawrence Erlbaum Associates, 1985), 43-82.

5. Herbert A. Simon, "Problem Solving and Education," in *Problem Solving and Education: Issues in Teaching and Research*, David T. Tuma and Frederick Reif,

eds. (Hillsdale, NJ: Lawrence Erlbaum Associates, 1980), 81-96; Robert Glaser, "Education and Thinking: The Role of Knowledge," *American Psychologist* 65 (1984): 93-104.

6. Robert J. Sternberg, "Intelligence as Thinking and Learning Skills," *Educational Leadership* 39 (1981): 18-20.

7. Stewart C. Purkey, *School Improvement: An Analysis of an Urban School District Effective Schools Project* (Madison, WI: Wisconsin Center for Educational Research, 1984), 1-9; Stewart C. Purkey and Susan Degen, "Beyond Effective Schools to Good Schools: Some First Steps," in *R&D Perspectives* (Eugene, OR: Center for Educational Policy and Management, University of Oregon, 1985).

8. John S. Brown, "Idea Amplifiers—New Kinds of Electronic Learning Environments," *educational HORIZONS* 63 (1981): 108-112.

9. Linda Darling-Hammond, "Mad-Hatter Tests of Good Teaching," *New York Times*, 8 January 1984, p. 57.

10. Sternberg, "Intelligence as Thinking and Learning Skills," 18-20.

11. David Pratt, *Curriculum Design and Development* (New York: Harcourt, Brace, Jovanovich, 1980), 303.

12. Jean Piaget, in *Piaget's Theory in Carmichael's Manual of Child Psychology*, vol. 1, Paul H. Mussen, ed. (New York: John Wiley, 1970), 703-732.

13. Gerald W. Bracey, "On the Compelling Need to Go Beyond Minimum Competency," *Phi Delta KAPPAN* 64 (1983): 717-721.

14. Barry K. Beyer, "Teaching Thinking Skills: How the Principal Can Know They Are Being Taught," *NASSP Bulletin* 69 (1985): 70-83.

15. Barbara Z. Presseisen, *Unlearned Lessons: Current and Past Reforms for School Improvement* (Philadelphia and London: Falmer Press, 1985).

16. Francis P. Hunkins, "A Systematic Model for Curriculum Development," *NASSP Bulletin* 69 (1985): 23-27.

17. Center for Performance Assessment, "Developing Good Tests: The 5x8 Card Makes It Easier," *Captrends* 10 (1985): 1-3.

18. Paul Berman and Milbrey McLaughlin, *Federal Programs Supporting Educational Change*, vol. 3, *Implementing and Sustaining Innovations*, R-1589/8-HEW (Santa Monica: CA: RAND Corporation, 1978).

19. Donald W. Dorr-Bremme, "Assessing Students: Teachers' Routine Practices and Reasonings," *Evaluation Comment* 8 (1983): 10.

20. Ann Lieberman, "The Curriculum Reform Debate: Some Critical Issues," *Teachers College Record* 85 (1984): 663-670.

21. Purkey and Degen, "Beyond Effective Schools," 2.

22. Presseisen, *Unlearned Lessons*, 119-124.

23. William Honig, "The Educational Excellence Movement: Now Comes the Hard Part," *Phi Delta KAPPAN* 66 (1985): 678.

24. Peter Kneedler, *A Practical Workshop on the Critical Thinking Skills in Social Studies* (Sacramento, CA: California Assessment Program, 1984), 1-45.

25. National Science Board Commission, *Educating Americans for the 21st Century: A Plan of Action for Improving Mathematics, Science and Technology Education for all American Elementary and Secondary Students So That Their Achievement Is the Best in the World by 1995* (Washington, D.C.: National Science Board Commission on Precollegiate Education in Mathematics, Science and Technology, National Science Foundation, 1983).

4

SELECTED
RESOURCE GUIDE

Education in the 20th century is marked by the growing importance of varied media for classroom instruction. Until the turn of the century, chalk, the hand-carried slate, and a few textbooks like *McGuffey's Eclectic Readers*, were the student's only educational materials. Today's multimedia, including audio, video, and computer technology, are relatively recent additions to the school's instructional paraphernalia, providing a virtual smorgasbord for the classroom teacher. The important question is, Which type of resource meets the needs of the students and provides an appropriate experience worthy of classroom time?

Whenever one raises the question of whether a particular thing should be done, one should consider whether it is better to do the thing in question than the other things that might be done in the same time. It is not a matter of the advantages of doing something rather than nothing; it is a matter of how best to allocate limited resources and, in particular, limited time. In judging the merits of any educational program (or materials) then, one must consider not only its benefits relative to its costs, but in estimating its costs, one must include not only the direct costs involved in effecting that program but also the opportunity costs, i.e., the opportunities for other types of instruction that are lost by virtue of the time and resources that are devoted to the program in question.[1]

The purchase and use of one or several of the published thinking skills programs should occur only after a faculty has seriously examined the ways of thinking that students need to develop. Consideration of teachers' skills and interests are also important in making the selection to use a published program, because different published programs emphasize different thinking skills.[2] Some programs stress essential skills; others highlight one or more of the complex processes. Few programs address all the aspects of the program design proposed in this book or how to balance a curriculum that seeks to incorporate all of them. Nevertheless, knowledge of the various published programs for teaching thinking, in addition to knowledge of resources in general, is very important to the leadership of a thinking skills project. Teacher leaders, administrators, and supervisors should be well informed about them and their research bases.

It follows, then, that a bank of exemplary instructional materials must be available to the teachers responsible for developing the day-to-day activities of teaching thinking. Beyer proposes that a professional library of research studies, how-to-do-it articles, and instructional materials on the nature of teaching cognitive skills should be a regular part of a school's or district's services.[3] When exemplary materials are collected systematically, supervisors can refer to them to help teachers develop more effective lessons, and teachers then have a local resource to draw on for ongoing planning. Clearly, budgetary support for the development and maintenance of such a collection would demonstrate the school's commitment to the improved teaching of thinking. Just as obvious is the need to use such a collection; little improvement accrues from the accumulation of dust!

What would a resource collection for teaching thinking include? Apart from the references at the end of each chapter that speak to the conceptual bases of the program and which continue to be informative to the overall design, I have listed 16 additional topics that teachers will find useful when teaching thinking. Each topic includes illustrative examples of the kinds of materials that might be selected for that topic. These are not meant to be comprehensive; obviously, many items can be located for each topic and none is mutually exclusive. Nor is there an evaluative implication in the selection. Materials suggested for thinking skills instruction should, indeed, be examined and their usefulness judged, but that is not the goal of this task. Most important are the categories of thinking skill resources, because they suggest the range of information that a staff must be cognizant of in planning thinking skills instruction in terms of this design. Building a resource collection around these suggested topics is a challenging task. If done well, it can become the center of a successful thinking program.

The checklist for materials considered for teaching thinking (Appendix A) will also be useful. Pratt's list of learning resources and teaching methods is presented in Figure 10 and may also serve as a guide to the full range of possibilities toward which resources can be directed. The only thing he failed to list was a rebus as a particular kind of puzzle, and one most useful to modality interplay.

TOPIC AREAS FOR THINKING SKILLS INSTRUCTION (with exemplary materials)

1. Published Programs for Thinking Skills Instruction

    1.1 Instrumental Enrichment (Reuven Feuerstein).
Curriculum Development Associates
1211 Connecticut Avenue, N.W.
Suite 414
Washington, DC 20036

also,

    Scott, Foresman and Company
Lifelong Learning Division
1900 East Lake Avenue
Glenview, IL 60025

    1.2 Philosophy for Children (Matthew Lipman).
Institute for the Advancement of Philosophy for
    Children
Montclair State College
Upper Montclair, NJ 07043

    1.3 Strategic Reasoning.
Innovative Sciences, Inc.
Park Square Station
P.O. Box 15129
Stamford, CT 06901

2. Resources That Emphasize Essential Thinking Skills

    2.1 Howard Black and Sandra Black, *Building Thinking Skills*, series (Pacific Grove, CA: Midwest Publications, 1984).
Midwest Publications
P.O. Box 448
Pacific Grove, CA 93950-0448

    2.2 High Scope Resources for pre-school and primary grades.
High/Scope Press
600 North River Street
Ypsilanti, MI 48198

    2.3 Bryce B. Hudgins, *Learning and Thinking* (Itasca, IL: F.E. Peacock, 1977).

album	electric map	modeling	research paper
anecdote	essay exercise	montage	role playing
apprenticeship	exhibit	motion picture	
aquarium	experiment	movie	sandtable
artifact		photography	scrapbook
audio record	facsimile	mural	sculpture
	feel bag	museum	seminar
book	feltboard	music	silkscreen
brainstorming	field research		simulation
bulletin board	field trip	newspaper	sketch
	filmstrip	notebook	slide
card game	flashcards		transparency
cartoon	flow chart	opaque	song
case study		projection	source material
chalkboard	game	outdoors	sports
charade	globe	overhead	stamps & coins
chart	group project	transparency	sticker book
chip talk	guest		story
club		painting	student lecture
collage	hand calculator	pamphlet	survey
collection	holograph	panel	
coloring book		pantomime	tachistoscope
comic book	imitation	parents	task cards
community	improvisation	participant	teacher
competition	interview	observation	teacher aide
computer		pegboard	team competition
computer-based	jigsaw	photography	team teaching
instruction		play	telephone
cooking	kit	poem	telescope
correspondence		poster	television
crossword	laboratory	printing press	terrarium
cutout	language master	problem	test
	lecture	programmed	textbook
dance	library	instruction	time-lapse
data sheet		project	photography
debate	magazine	psychodrama	toy
demonstration	magnetic board	puppets	treasure hunt
design	map	puzzle	tutorial
diagram	microfilm		typewriter
dial-a-lecture	microfragrance	questionnaire	
dialogue	microscope	quiz	videotape
diary	mnemonic	quotation	vivarium
diorama	mobile		
discussion	mock trial	radio	word game
drama	model	real-life	workbook
drawing		experience	
drill		replica	

FIGURE 10. Pratt's Learning Resources and Teaching Methods

3. Resources that Emphasize Complex Thinking Skills

3.1 Cognitive Levels and Matching Project.
Dr. Martin Brooks
Shoreham-Wading River School District
Shoreham, NY 11786

3.2 Raymond S. Nickerson et al., *Odyssey: A Curriculum for Thinking* (Watertown, MA: Mastery Education, 1986).
Mastery Education
85 Main Street
Watertown, MA 02172

3.3 Arthur Whimbey, *Analytical Reading and Reasoning* (Stamford, CT: Innovative Sciences, 1983).

4. Resources that Emphasize Metacognitive Thinking Skills

4.1 Joseph D. Novak and D. Bob Gowin, *Learning How to Learn* (New York: Cambridge University Press, 1985).

4.2 D. Ray Reutzel, "Story Maps Improve Comprehension," *The Reading Teacher* 38 (1985): 400-404.

4.3 Steven R. Yussen, ed., *The Growth of Reflection in Children* (New York: Academic Press, 1985).

5. Resources that Elaborate Problem Solving

5.1 Linda J. Sheffield, *Problem Solving in Math* (New York: Scholastic Skill Books, 1982).

5.2 Franette Walberg, *Puzzle Thinking* (Philadelphia: Franklin Institute Press, 1980).

5.3 Arthur Whimbey and Jack Lochhead, *Problem Solving and Comprehension* (Philadelphia: Franklin Institute Press, 1982).

6. Resources that Elaborate Decision Making

6.1 Diane Draze, *OPTIONS: A Guide for Creative Decision Making* (San Luis Obispo, CA: Dandy Lion Publications, 1982).

6.2 Micki McKisson, *Chrysalis: Nurturing Creative and Independent Thought in Children* (Tucson, AZ: Zephyr Press Learning Materials, 1983).
Zephyr Press Learning Materials
430 S. Essex Lane
Tucson, AZ 85711

6.3 Judy Rierson and Mary Claiborne, *Extending Thinking Abilities*, no. 8112 (Buffalo, NY: D.O.K. Publishers, n.d.).
D.O.K. Publishers
71 Radcliff Road
Buffalo, NY 14213

7. Resources that Elaborate Critical Thinking

7.1 Diane F. Halpern, *Thought and Knowledge: An Introduction to Critical Thinking* (Hillsdale, NJ: Lawrence Erlbaum Associates, 1984).

7.2 Anita Harnadak, *Critical Thinking*, series (Pacific Grove, CA: Midwest Publications, 1976).
Midwest Publications
P.O. Box 448
Pacific Grove, CA 93950-0448

7.3 John E. McPeck, *Critical Thinking and Education* (Oxford, England: Martin Robertson and Company, 1981).

8. Resources that Elaborate Creative Thinking

8.1 Books that illustrate using language creatively such as:
Marvin Terban, *Eight Ate: A Feast of Homonym Riddles* (New York: Clarion Books, 1982).
Marvin Terban, *In a Pickle: And Other Funny Idioms* (New York: Clarion Books, 1983).

8.2 CoRT Materials, Edward deBono, Cognitive Research Trust.
Pergamon Press
Fairview Park
Elmsford, NY 10523

8.3 Sam Epstein and Beryl Epstein, *The First Book of Codes and Ciphers*, 1956.
Franklin Watts, Inc.
875 Lexington Avenue
New York, NY 10022

9. Resources that Apply Thinking to Language Arts

9.1 John N. Hays et al., *The Writer's Mind: Writing as a Mode of Thinking* (Urbana, IL: National Council of Teachers of English, 1985).

9.2 Charles Suhor, "Thinking Skills in the English Language Arts," *Problem Solving* 5 (1983): 1-4.

9.3 Twist-A-Plot Books.
Scholastic, Inc.
730 Broadway
New York, NY 10003

10. Resources that Apply Thinking to Mathematics

10.1 Sun Jin Pai and Hang Young Pai, *Chisanbop: Original Finger Calculation* (New York, NY: American Book Company, 1984).
American Book Company
135 W. 50th Street
New York, NY 10020

10.2 Nuffield Mathematics Project.
John Wiley and Sons, Inc.
605 Third Avenue
New York, NY 10158

10.3 Steven S. Willoughby et al., *Real Math* (LaSalle, IL: Open Court
Mathematics and Science, 1985).
Open Court Publishing Company
P.O. Box 599
Pern, IL 61354-0599

11. Resources that Apply Thinking to Social Studies

11.1 Catherine Cornbleth, "Critical Thinking and Cognitive Process,"
in *Review of Research in Social Studies Education 1976-1983*,
bulletin 75 (1983), 11-63.

11.2 Maps, documents, vocabulary, writing, tests.
Educational Masterprints Company
Box 269
Garden City, Long Island
New York, NY 11530

11.3 Jamieson McKenzie, "In Search of a Scope and Sequence for
Social Studies," *Social Education* 48 (1984): 249-261.

12. Resources that Apply Thinking to Science

12.1 Arnold B. Arons, "Computer-Based Instructional Dialogues in
Science Courses," *Science* 224 (1984): 1056.

12.2 Anton E. Lawson, "Investigating and Applying Developmental Psychology in the Science Classroom," in *Learning and Motivation in the Classroom*, Scott Paris, Gary M. Olson, Harold
W. Stevenson, eds. (Hillsdale, NJ: Lawrence Erlbaum, 1983),
113-135.

12.3 Lawrence A. Stevens, *Thinking Tools: A Young Person's Guide
to Problem Solving* (Stockton, CA: Stevens and Shea Publishers, n.d.).
Stevens and Shea Publishers
325 E. Wyandotte Street
Stockton, CA 95204

13. Resources that Apply Thinking to the Arts

13.1 Betty Edwards, *Drawing on the Right Side of the Brain* (Los
Angeles: J.P. Tarcher, Inc., distributed by Houghton Mifflin
Company, 1979).

13.2 Laura Chapman, *Discover Art*, series (Worcester, MA: Davis
Publications, 1985).

13.3 Jon J. Murray, "Art, Creativity, and the Quality of Education,"
Independent School 43 (1984): 23-27, 60-66.

13.4 Mona Brookes, *Drawing with Children* (Los Angeles: J.P. Tarcher, Inc., distributed by St. Martin's Press, 1986).

14. Resources that Apply Thinking to Computer Science

14.1 Beverly Hunter, *My Students Use Computers: Learning Activities for Computer Literacy* (Reston, VA: Reston Publishing Company, 1983).

14.2 Peter H. Martorella, "Interactive Video Systems in the Classroom," *Social Education* 47 (1983): 325-327.

14.3 Writing to Read System.
International Business Machines
IBM Building—Room 600 A&B
100 E. Pratt Street
Baltimore, MD 21202

15. Testing and Assessment Materials

15.1 Cognitive Abilities Test (CogAT).
The Riverside Publishing Company
8420 Bryn Mawr Avenue
Chicago, IL 60631

15.2 Robert Ennis and Jason Millman, *Cornell Critical Thinking Test, Level X* (Pacific Grove, CA: Midwest Publications, 1985).
Midwest Publications
P.O. Box 448
Pacific Grove, CA 93950-0448

15.3 Goodwin Watson and Edward M. Glaser, *Watson-Glaser, Critical Thinking Appraisal*, Forms A&B (Cleveland, OH: Psychological Corporation, 1980).
Psychological Corporation
Subsidiary of Harcourt Brace and Jovanovich
7500 Old Oak Boulevard
Cleveland, OH 44130

16. Teacher Planning Materials for Curriculum and Instruction

16.1 Hans G. Furth and Harry Wachs, *Thinking Goes to School: Piaget's Theory in Practice* (New York: Oxford University Press, 1974).

16.2 ASCD Resource Materials and Study Institutes (print, audio, and video materials).
Association for Supervision and Curriculum
  Development
125 North West Street
Alexandria, VA 22314

16.3 ASCD Thinking Skills Network (newsletter and directory).
Dr. John Barell

210 Chapin Hall
Montclair State College
Upper Montclair, NJ 07043

Because these programs vary in regard to their theoretical underpinnings, the thinking skills upon which they focus, the teaching methods they utilize, and their implementation requirements.
The following questions should be considered when examining all
programs and materials.

1. Is the program based on a theoretical model?
2. What thinking skills are identified, developed, and evaluated
   by the program?
3. Are the identified thinking skills explicitly taught or are they
   imbedded within the curriculum?
4. What is the target population of the program (grade level, subject area, ability level)?
5. What is the teacher's role in implementing the program? What
   instructional methods are employed?
6. What instructional materials are required? What supplemen-
   tary materials are available?
7. What are the teacher training requirements? Are training services available?
8. What are the implementation and maintenance costs for the
   program? What are the per pupil costs?
9. How has the program been evaluated? What is the evidence
   of its effectiveness?
10. Is the program being conducted at a nearby school? What is
    the name of a contact person who could answer questions
    and/or arrange for an observation visit?*

*Adapted from the work of Jay McTighe, Maryland Department of Education,
1986, used with permission of the author.

---

1. Raymond S. Nickerson et al., *The Teaching of Learning Strategies* (Cambridge,
MA: Bolt, Beranek, and Newman, 1984), 135.

2. Barbara Z. Presseisen, "Thinking Skills: Meanings and Models," in *Developing Minds: A Resource Book for Teaching Thinking*, Arthur L. Costa, ed. (Alexandria, VA: Association for Supervision and Curriculum Development, 1985),
43-48.

3. Barry K. Beyer, "Teaching Thinking Skills: How the Principal Can Know They
Are Being Taught," *NASSP Bulletin* (1985): 81.

PUTTING THE DESIGN TO WORK

Developing a specific program design for teaching thinking forces the educator to examine many program options and to assess them for potential benefit in the long-term curriculum. The experience of developing the design presented here should elicit answers to the following questions:

- Should there be a separate thinking skills course?
- Should a particular published program or programs for thinking be adopted or adapted to specific classrooms?
- Should thinking skills instruction be included throughout the existing curriculum?

A separate course on thinking could be developed. Time could be allotted to teaching thinking as a particular subject area. Such an arrangement would certainly highlight the specific processes of thinking stressed in the instruction and would probably elucidate the metacognitive operations as well. In curriculum development, however, the separate course approach may be effective for immediate remedial outcomes but generally fails as a long-lasting curricular improvement.[1] Teachers resist pressures to expand already extensive course offerings. Even more critical is the lack of a teacher constituency for teaching thinking as a separate subject matter. Teachers are interested in cognitive development, but they prefer to approach it through the content or the grade level, which they consider their personal expertise. When linked to everyday curriculum and to regular instructional tasks, teaching thinking can be significant to a teaching staff and foster common bonds with other disciplines or across the school's general program. Buying a published program for teaching thinking is probably the most expeditious way to move quickly into thinking skills instruction. Some very creative programs for teaching thinking are currently available (see the Materials Guide in Chapter 4), and some of them offer teacher preparation packages that have been judged effective.[2] However, as I have suggested, few of these programs are comprehensive in their design. Most concentrate on only one or two of the complex processes of thinking and in limited subject matter; almost none consider the development of thought processes from kindergarten through high school. Only some of the published programs are explicitly tied to specific course content; and, they offer few links to other subject matters. Adopting such programs as the only means of teaching thinking in the curriculum will probably result in limited and fragmented improvement. Curricular leadership will be required to help a staff see the importance of a thinking skills approach in their entire instructional endeavor.

Including thinking skills throughout the entire K-12 curriculum is a main thrust of this program design. Thinking is not an "add-on" to the school's program, a subject matter to be included or removed as the whim arises. Nor is thinking merely to be "caught" as regular content is "covered." Thinking is the *raison d'être* of schooling. Young people must develop higher order cognitive processes required in today's technological world. Without them, the learning deficit will continue for a lifetime. It is equally important that all instructional departments in elementary and secondary schooling see thinking skills and processes as their common concern, because these are the building blocks of a cohesive school program. From setting the objectives to selecting textbooks or making daily lesson plans, thinking should be a high priority in curriculum development.

The proposed design and its implementation plan highlight four important aspects that are major contributors to a successful comprehensive thinking skills program:

- the importance of early and continued intervention in thinking;
- the significance of intrinsic motivation;
- the potential of metacognitive learning; and
- the challenge of multiple modalities.

Children, even in pre-school years, have the ability to think, to make certain discriminations, to develop memory and perceptual skills.[3] That ability requires specific instruction in the early grades. In fact, for disadvantaged children, some say this may be the most critical period.[4] Many of the reform reports advocate early intervention of cognitive development in specific content areas.[5] Other thinking skills specialists call for the continued role of specific intervention in teaching thinking, regularly offered content-free or content-incidental instruction that explicitly teaches students how to think and what thinking is about.[6]

There is an emphasis on intrinsic motivation that also emerges in the teaching of thinking. Both the constructivist instructional strategy and the sheer enjoyment of working out problems or solutions in meaningful ways help make learning a positive experience for students and for teachers. Researchers in video game technology are mindful of Adler's charge that youngsters are curious when they come to school, but that they often lose their curiosity in dull instructional environments.[7] The need to build a thinking skills program that stimulates learners intellectually and challenges them continuously is tied to the very precepts of a thinking skills curriculum. Keeping the student's interest paramount in the mediation is key to responding to the motivational task. As Gardner suggests, educators should remind themselves,

> Musically inclined preschoolers . . . easily learned to play simple instruments not only because they found musical patterns easy to learn, but because they found them almost impossible to forget.[8]

The role of metacognitive thinking must also be emphasized as an important aspect of the program design, in which the complexity of human thinking and its development is underlined. The growing significance of heuristics and tacit knowledge are as important to the development of higher order skills as to problem solving and critical thinking. This places greater emphasis on the teacher's professional expertise in particular content areas, and assumes capability for working with students on basic skill remediation within the context of subject matter. This emphasis also raises concern for developing dispositions and study skill routines over the learner's entire academic career and suggests that articulation among staff, especially between levels of schooling, is a necessity for sound instruction.

Finally, the challenge of dealing with multiple modalities in the school's curriculum becomes an important aspect of building a comprehensive thinking skills program. American schooling has long focused on linguistic and quantitative modes of thought, but now, with the advent of television and video technology, the importance of spatial-visual understanding has become more of an issue in learning. There is now some concern that high school seniors' visual skills have declined alarmingly.[9] Concern for figurative and symbolic understanding may partially explain why students taking the recent NAEP reading tests have not progressed in higher order cognitive development.[10] Recent advances in teaching writing to young students indicate that youngsters with ideational fluency, often inspired by the use of multiple modes of perception, do better at both writing and test performance.[11] These issues raise questions about how modalities are handled in the curriculum. To conceive of thinking skills only as the prerogative of so-called academic courses—language arts, science, mathematics, and social studies—may create a serious deficit in terms of the potential contributions of the arts including graphic, performance, and industrial studies, to students' understanding. It seems that the more modalities are interrelated, the greater the opportunities for an interdisciplinary base to the overall curriculum.

Developing the program design proposed here focuses on basic requirements of a sound thinking skills program. These requirements can be clearly seen when the dimensions of the program are clarified.

- Teachers and administrators must work together to build a sound thinking skills curriculum. Time and funds need to be provided to make this collaborative effort possible.
- Teachers and administrators need to take a serious look at the existing school program and consider which thinking skills can help improve instruction as well as content development in that program.
- Teachers and administrators need to work together to create or adapt classroom experiences, including testing, to help students improve their cognitive performance through a better understanding of and more practice at thinking skills development.

There are several factors that can deter the establishment of a sound thinking skills program. Time and money may not be available. Understanding the fine points of a particular curriculum or a specialized subject matter requires teachers who are well prepared in academic fields. Most important of all, thinking may be little valued in a community, even by the educators themselves. This suggests that the social leveling process sometimes associated with television and fast food chains is also possible in schooling. How odd that the richest nation in the world—with more books, more teachers, more computers—could be subject to what Perkins calls "the dark side of the fingertip effect."[12] Educators are encouraged to start work in their own schools and districts to assess what is needed in terms of thinking skills and to build on the curriculum that already exists (see Appendices E and F for a sample survey instrument and a district's model skills continuum K-12).

There is at the base of the thinking skills movement a question about how schooling is related to preserving and upgrading the culture of a society. Those involved in the thinking skills movement see it even more broadly as incorporating the perceptual and kinaesthetic beginnings that shape thought itself.[13] I submit that the practice of schooling is intimately involved with preserving the essence of civilization. Epstein suggests that the patterns of improved thinking—the higher order skills which are examined here—in fact, can be reversed.[14] He maintains that the Third Reich sought to reduce symbolic thought to banal existence, mindlessness, and a life without imagination. That may seem dramatic and overdrawn, but it is a possible explanation to consider in terms of understanding teacher malaise and educational frustration in contemporary society.

Schools are invaluable to a society, not because they are the repositories of accumulated information to be spoon fed to young students, but because they are institutions that teach the skills that make generating knowledge possible. Teaching thinking is far from a momentary fad. The recurring challenge is to prepare each generation to think for itself and every student to reach his or her highest potential.

---

1. Michael Kirst and Gail R. Meister, "Turbulence in American Secondary Schools: What Reforms Last?" *Curriculum Inquiry* 15 (1985): 169-186.

2. Robert J. Sternberg, "How Can We Teach Intelligence?" *Educational Leadership* 42 (1984): 38-39.

3. John R. Berrueta-Clement et al., *Changed Lives: The Effects of the Perry Preschool Program on Youths Through Age 19* (Ypsilanti, MI: High/Scope Press, 1984).

4. Council for Economic Development, *Investing in Our Children* (New York: Council for Economic Development, 1985).

5. National Science Board Commission, *Educating Americans for the 21st Century: A Plan of Action for Improving Mathematics, Science and Technology Education for All American Elementary and Secondary Students So That Their Achievement Is the Best in the World by 1995* (Washington, D.C.: National Science Board Commission on Precollegiate Education in Mathematics, Science and Technology, National Science Foundation, 1983).

6. Barry K. Beyer, "What's in a Skill? Defining the Thinking Skills We Teach," *Social Science Review* 24 (1984): 19-23; Barry K. Beyer, "Critical Thinking Revisit-

ed," *Social Education* 49 (1985): 268-302; Raymond S. Nickerson, "Thoughts on Teaching Thinking," *Educational Leadership* 39 (1981): 21-24.

7. Mortimer J. Adler, *The Paideia Proposal: An Educational Manifesto* (New York: Macmillan, 1982).

8. Kevin McKean, "Intelligence: New Ways to Measure the Wisdom of Man," *Discover* 6 (1985): 28.

9. Thomas L. Hilton, *National Changes in Spatial-Visual Ability from 1960-1980* (Princeton, NJ: Educational Testing Service, 1985).

10. Gene I. Maeroff, "Student Reading Held Its Level for 14 Years, Federal Survey Finds," *New York Times*, 19 September 1985, p. A16; Lynn Olson, "Reading Skills Up but Leveling Off, Report Finds," *Education Week*, 25 September 1986, pp. 1, 17.

11. Fred M. Hechinger, "Making 'a Lot of Words' Tell a Story," *New York Times*, 10 September 1985, p. C7.

12. David N. Perkins, "The Fingertip Effect: How Information Processing Technology Shapes Thinking," *Educational Researcher* 14 (1985): 11-17.

13. David R. Olson, "Culture, Technology, and Intellect," in *The Nature of Intelligence*, Lauren B. Resnick, ed. (Hillsdale, NJ: Lawrence Erlbaum Associates, 1976), 189-202.

14. Leslie Epstein, "Atrocity and Imagination," *Harper's* 271 (1985): 13-16.

APPENDIX A

Resource Title _____

Author(s)_____

Producer/Publisher _____ Date _____

Pages/Disks_____Medium_____

Grade Level _____

Content Area_____

Directions: Circle the number of the response you consider most appropriate for each item below.

| 5 = Excellent | 4 = Good | 3 = Average | 2 = Fair | 1 = Poor |

1. Materials help define or delimit a particular skill (specify skill below).

   _____ 5 4 3 2 1
   _____ 5 4 3 2 1
   _____ 5 4 3 2 1

2. Materials help develop the model form for instructing a particular skill (specify skill below).

   _____ 5 4 3 2 1
   _____ 5 4 3 2 1
   _____ 5 4 3 2 1

3. Materials are conducive to student use with peer interaction while practicing a skill (specify skill below).

   _____ 5 4 3 2 1
   _____ 5 4 3 2 1
   _____ 5 4 3 2 1

4. Materials enable student to practice skill independently (specify skill below).

   _____ 5 4 3 2 1
   _____ 5 4 3 2 1
   _____ 5 4 3 2 1

5. Materials enable student to practice skill
   heuristically (specify skill below).

   _____   5   4   3   2   1
   _____   5   4   3   2   1
   _____   5   4   3   2   1

6. Materials provide adequate assessment of
   specific thinking skills (specify skill below).

   _____   5   4   3   2   1
   _____   5   4   3   2   1
   _____   5   4   3   2   1

7. Materials provide for appropriate cognitive
   development level of students being in-
   structed (specify skill below).

   pre-operational level   5   4   3   2   1
   concrete operational level   5   4   3   2   1
   formal operational level   5   4   3   2   1

APPENDIX B

THINKING SKILLS LESSON PLAN

Teacher ____ G. Jones ____

School ____ Hubbard Elementary ____ Grade ____ 4 ____

Course ____ Science ____ Date(s) ____ October 9,10 ____

Lesson/Topic ____ Physical and Chemical Change ____

Content/ Resources	Pupil Performance Objective(s)	Methods/Activities	Thinking Skills and Related Information
I. Content: Changes in Nature A. Physical B. Chemical	I. The pupil will be able to differentiate between a physical and a chemical change by: A. Constructing his or her own definition of each. B. Citing at least 5 examples of each kind of change.	I. Introduction of Concept: Change A. Key Questions 1. What do you think of when you speak of change? 2. Select any object or organism and list or show the different ways it could change. 3. How do we know that something has changed? 4. What do you think a physical change is? A chemical change?	Prior Knowledge-Qualifications Classification/Comparison Analysis-Relationships Transformation

THINKING SKILLS LESSON PLAN

Teacher __G. Jones__   Course __Science__   Date(s) __October 9,10__

School __Hubbard Elementary__   Grade __4__   Lesson/Topic __Physical and Chemical Change__

Content/Resources	Pupil Performance Objective(s)	Methods/Activities	Thinking Skills and Related Information

II. Resources:
 	
A. Text(s)___
B. Demonstration Items
C. Worksheets
		II. Silent Demonstration by Teacher
		Directions for Student Processing
		
		A. You will now observe a series of ten demonstrations of changes; the first five will be physical changes; the last five will be chemical changes.
		
		1. Observe carefully.
		2. Note or draw your observation on your worksheet — part 1.
		3. Form small discussion groups and consider:
		  a. How was each object changed?
		  b. What actually did change?
		
		In your group, try to arrive at a common definition of a physical and chemical change.
			
			Observation-Qualification
			Classification
			
			Analysis
			Analysis
			
			Generalization

THINKING SKILLS LESSON PLAN

Teacher ___G. Jones___

School ___Hubbard Elementary___ Grade ___4___

Course ___Science___ Date(s) ___October 9,10___

Lesson/Topic ___Physical and Chemical Change___

Content/ Resources	Pupil Performance Objective(s)	Methods/Activities	Thinking Skills and Related Information
		4. Complete parts 2, 3, and 4 on your worksheet by yourself.	
		a. Review in words or symbols how objects changed — part 2.	Expressive-Modality Shift
		b. Tell or show your own definition of a physical and a chemical change — part 3.	Deduction
		5. Was this assignment easy, medium, or hard? Mark the box in part 4. Tell why. How would you do it next time?	Judgment/Causation
			Metacognitive Reflection

APPENDIX C

A GENERAL TEACHING ALGORITHM

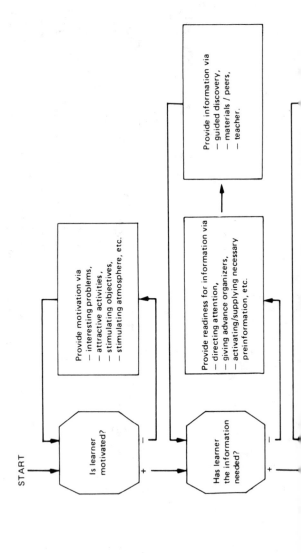

START

Is learner motivated?

Provide motivation via
— interesting problems,
— attractive activities,
— stimulating objectives,
— stimulating atmosphere, etc.

Has learner the information needed?

Provide readiness for information via
— directing attention,
— giving advance organizers,
— activating/supplying necessary preinformation, etc.

Provide information via
— guided discovery,
— materials / peers,
— teacher.

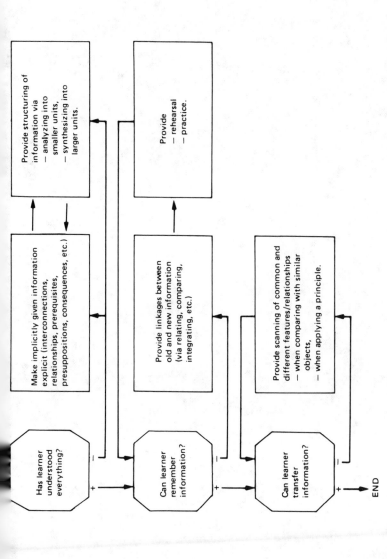

From "Framework for a Theory of Teaching," by Karl J. Klauer, *Teaching and Teacher Education* 1 (1985), reprinted by permission of Pergamon Books Ltd.

APPENDIX D

STUDENT CURRICULUM EVALUATION FORM

YES NO   Comments

☐ ☐   1. Do you believe the goals and objectives of this class are important and worthwhile to you?

☐ ☐   2. Are the materials we use interesting, usable, and in ample supply?

☐ ☐   3. Is the content of this unit (or lesson) important, understandable, and worthwhile to you now? Will it be useful to you in the future?   _____

_____

☐ ☐   4. Are the activities we engage in helpful to you in achieving the goals and objectives of this course? Are they interesting and stimulating or boring and repetitive?   _____

_____

_____

☐ ☐   5. Am I able to facilitate your learning by what I do when I teach? What teaching strategies help you learn best?

☐ ☐   Lecture
☐ ☐   Discussion
☐ ☐   Role play
☐ ☐   Simulations
☐ ☐   Media presentations
☐ ☐   Text assignments
☐ ☐   Small group sessions

☐ ☐   6. What forms of evaluation do you think would be more useful to you — self-evaluation, group evaluations, or teacher evaluation for projects? How do you feel when you have to take tests often?

☐ ☐   7. How do you like the group you currently are working with? Do you think you were placed fairly for instructional purposes? Do you prefer working as a class, in small groups, or individually?   _____

_____

_____

☐ ☐   8. Do you believe you are using your
          time wisely in this class? Would you   _____
          like more time for independent work
          on your interests? Would you like to   _____
          have our class time shortened or ex-
          tended?   _____

☐ ☐   9. Do you like the physical arrange-   _____
          ment of our classroom? Would
          desks or tables and chairs better   _____
          facilitate our work? Is the space we
          have available adequate for our   _____
          classroom activities?

From "The Use of a Research Model to Guide Curriculum Development," pp.
201-202, by M. Frances Klein, *Theory Into Practice* 22 (1983).

APPENDIX E

THINKING SKILLS THROUGHOUT THE K-12
CURRICULUM A THOUGHTFUL APPRAISAL

TYPICALLY,
I. DOES YOUR SCHOOL COMMUNITY. . .

YES NO

☐ ☐ 1. Value thinking as a primary goal of education for *all* students?

☐ ☐ 2. Have an expectation that all students can enhance their intelligence by appropriate learning and experience?

☐ ☐ 3. Agree on major thinking skills/processes that are the basis of the school's program and provide an updated document to share this agreement among all staff?

☐ ☐ 4. Arrange learning activities in order of increasing complexity and greater abstraction across various grade levels and among different disciplines?

☐ ☐ 5. Organize instruction around a variety of modalities and thinking-oriented materials?

☐ ☐ 6. Encourage teachers to plan cooperatively for thinking instruction across the K-12 program?

☐ ☐ 7. Provide inservice or staff development to help teachers improve the inclusion of thinking throughout the school program?

☐ ☐ 8. Assess student growth of various thinking abilities and use results of such assessment in future planning and development?

☐ ☐ 9. Provide for the regular review and acquisition of thinking-oriented materials?

II. IN YOUR CLASSROOM, DO YOU. . .

☐ ☐ 10. Use thinking skills as a base for lesson planning and development?

☐ ☐ 11. Teach thinking skills directly and carefully follow up on student application and practice?

☐ ☐ 12. Encourage students to reflect on thinking processes and share insights with their classmates?

☐ ☐   13. Look for sources of student's error in work completed incorrectly or inadequately?

☐ ☐   14. Enable better classroom performers to model skills for classmates and/or share effective strategies for learning?

☐ ☐   15. Vary your questioning technique or discussion guidance according to student response?

☐ ☐   16. Encourage students to help develop teaching and testing approaches?

☐ ☐   17. Reflect on your own instructional approaches and change them for greater teaching impact?

☐ ☐   18. Ask other teachers to share thinking-oriented insights/experiences with you?

III. DO YOUR STUDENTS. . .

☐ ☐   19. Settle down to work routines quickly?

☐ ☐   20. Question or ask for additional information spontaneously?

☐ ☐   21. Reply to direct questions with relevant and complete answers?

☐ ☐   22. Check or proofread their work without a request to do so?

☐ ☐   23. Take responsibility for make up assignments on their own?

☐ ☐   24. Look for different or alternate ways to solve problems?

☐ ☐   25. Show enthusiasm for solving problems about unknown contents or new materials?

From *Thinking Skills Academy,* Cooperative Schools Improvement Program (Philadelphia: Research for Better Schools, 1986).

References

Barry K. Beyer, "Teaching Thinking Skills: How the Principal can Know They Are Being Taught," *NASSP Bulletin* 69 (1985): 70-83.

Arthur L. Costa, "Mediating the Metacognitive," *Educational Leadership* 42 (1984): 57-62.

Reuven Feuerstein, *Instrumental Enrichment,* Teacher Observation Checklist (Washington, D.C.: Curriculum Development Associates, 1981).

APPENDIX F

A MODEL OF THINKING SKILLS: A BASIC PROCESSES CONTINUUM PRE K-12*

BALTIMORE CITY PUBLIC SCHOOLS THINKING SKILLS PROGRAM

Qualifications — basic identity; definition facts, problem/task recognition	Classifications — similarities and differences, either/or distinctions		Relationships — part/whole, patterns, sequences/order/logic deductions	Transformation — analogies, logical inductions	Causation — predictions, evaluation
Knowledge	Comprehension	Application	Analysis	Synthesis	Evaluation
12			Identifying and clarifying problems	Integrating knowledge and process from diverse areas	Evaluating strategies for problem solving, decision making and critical analysis
11			Collecting, organizing, and applying relevant evidence, analyzing systems; i.e. economic, syntactic, scientific	Formulating conclusions	Evaluating evidence
10			Analyzing informations: for example — distinguishing among causal, contingent, correlated relationships	Generating alternatives	Evaluating solutions: Relating premises to conclusions

	Qualifications basic identity; definition facts, problem/task recognition	Classifications similarities and differences, either/or distinctions		Relationships part/whole, patterns, sequences/order/logic deductions	Transformation analogies logical inductions	Causation predictions evaluation
	Knowledge	*Comprehension*	*Application*	*Analysis*	*Synthesis*	*Evaluation*
9				Interpreting information: relating, taking apart	Stating problems and/or constructing analogies/ hypotheses	Justifying conclusion Choosing alternative conclusions
8			Testing hypotheses: experimenting		Developing models	Devising alternative tests for hypotheses
7				Drawing logical conclusions	Generalizing	
				Identifying variables: Describing relationships among them; Predicting outcomes		
6	Collecting and organizing information —Identifying —Delining —Describing	—Interpreting —Comparing		Interpreting/Reporting Information		Evaluating Inferences
5	collecting, processing, demonstrating information	summarizing		differentiating		
4					recognizing more complex analogous relationships	

		interpreting	problem solving	predicting
3				
2		translating	recognizing part/whole relationships	recognizing simple analogous relationships
1			recognizing similarities and differences	deciding
K	examining, characterizing	grouping sorting	classifying	
Pre-K	recognizing, labeling		ordering	

*Based on Bloom's Cognitive Domain of Educational Objectives and the Presseisen Model of Thinking Skills.

Developed by the Thinking Skills Program Curriculum Subcommittee representing the Offices of Pre K-2, Cluster I, Cluster II, GATE; Fine Arts, Foreign Language, Language Arts, Mathematics, Science, Social Studies, Special Education, and Vocational Programs.

A GLOSSARY
OF THINKING
TERMS

Although there is no one glossary of thinking terms that serves the many nuances of meaning associated with cognitive operations, a working definition is a useful basis for understanding. The following terms and their definitions are drawn from the discussion in *Thinking Skills: Meanings and Models*, in the hope that they will provide some guidance to practitioners who seek to integrate thinking skills into their curricular and instructional tasks.

ALGORITHM. A problem solving procedure that, if followed exactly, will always yield the solution to a particular problem; compare with heuristic.

AMBIGUITY. When there is more than one meaning or underlying representation in a communication or utterance.

ANALOGY. A problem solving strategy in which linguistic or figural similarities are noted between two or more situations, while simultaneously discerning that there are also differences in the relationship.

ANALYSIS. Separation of a whole into its component parts.

BRAINSTORMING. A group or individual method for generating solution paths for problems; the goal is to produce multiple possible solutions.

CAUSATION. The act or process that occasions or effects a result.

CLASSIFICATION. To sort objects, events, or people into clusters according to their common factors or characteristics.

COGNITION. Related to the various thinking processes characteristic of human intelligence.

CATEGORICAL REASONING. Also known as syllogistic reasoning; use of such quantifiers as "some," "all," "no," and "none" to indicate category membership.

COMPARISON. Juxtaposing items to establish similarities and dissimilarities.

COMPREHENSION. The arrival at the speaker's/writer's intended meaning by a listener/reader.

CONCLUSION. An inferential belief that is derived from premises.

CONDITIONAL LOGIC. Also known as propositional logic; logical statements that are expressed in an "if, then" format.

CONTRASTING. To set objects or ideas in opposition or to compare them by emphasizing their differences.

CONSEQUENT. In "if, then" statements, it is the information given in the "then" clause.

CONTINGENCY RELATIONSHIP. Relationships that are expressed with "if, then" statements; the consequent is contingent or dependent upon the antecedent.

CONTRADICTION. A problem-solving strategy in which the problem solver shows that a goal cannot be obtained from the givens because of inconsistencies.

CONVERGENT THINKING. The kind of thinking in which you are required to come up with a single correct answer to a question or problem; compare with divergent thinking.

CREATIVE THINKING. Using basic thinking processes to develop or invent novel, aesthetic, constructive ideas or products.

CRITICAL THINKING. Using basic thinking processes to analyze arguments and generate insight into particular meanings and interpretations; also known as directed thinking.

DECISION MAKING. Using basic thinking processes to choose a best response among several options.

DEDUCTIVE REASONING. Use of stated premises to formulate conclusions that can logically be inferred from them.

DIVERGENT THINKING. The kind of thinking required when a person needs to generate many different responses to the same question or problem; compare with convergent thinking.

EPISTEMIC COGNITION. Related to the collective knowledge produced by thinking and the development and extension of this body of information.

ERROR. Something produced by mistake.

ESTIMATING. To form a judgment about worth, quantity, or significance on rather rough calculations.

EVALUATION. To make an examination or judgment.

EXTRAPOLATION. The estimation of a value from a trend suggested by known values.

FALLACY. An error or mistake in the thinking process.

GENERALIZATION. A problem solving strategy in which the problem is considered as an example of a larger class of problems; using the results obtained in a sample to infer that similar results would be obtained for a larger population if all cases or situations were assessed.

HEURISTIC. A general strategy or "rule of thumb" that is used to solve problems and make decisions; while it doesn't always produce a correct answer, it is usually a helpful aid; compare with algorithm.

HYPOTHESIS. A set of beliefs about the nature of the world, usually concerning the relationships between two or more variables.

HYPOTHESIZE. To construct tentative assumptions that appear to account for observed effect or conditions.

IDENTITY. A sameness of essential or generic characteristics.

ILLOGICAL. Reaching conclusions that are not in accord with the rules of logic.

INDUCTIVE REASONING. Making observations that suggest or lead to the formulation of a conclusion or hypothesis.

INFER. To derive as a conclusion from facts or premises; to guess, surmise.

INQUIRY. Seeking information about a problem or condition.

INSIGHT. Sudden knowledge of a solution to a problem.

INTERPRETATION. Explanation of the meaning of a situation or condition.

INTUITION. The power or faculty of attaining to direct knowledge or cognition without rational thought and inference.

JUDGMENT. The process of forming an opinion or evaluation.

KNOWLEDGE. The fact or condition of having information or of being learned.

LATERAL THINKING. Thinking "around" a problem; used to generate new ideas; compare with vertical thinking.

LOGICAL. Reaching conclusions that are in accord with the rules of logic, that is derived from valid (correct) conclusions.

MEMORY. The power or process of reproducing or recalling what has been learned and retained.

METACOGNITION. Related to how humans acquire thinking processes and are enabled to use those processes; conscious knowledge about our memory and thought processes.

METAPHOR. Linguistic comparisons formed when we note similarities between things that are basically dissimilar, often used in creative thinking.

MNEMONICS. Memory aids or techniques that are utilized to improve memory.

ORDERING OBJECTS. To arrange according to predetermined criteria.

PATTERN. An artistic or mechanical design revealing constant traits or replicable characteristics.

PERCEPTION. Awareness of the elements of environment through physical sensation.

PREDICTION. Foretelling on the basis of observation, experience, or scientific reason.

PREMISES. Statements that allow the inference of logical conclusions.

PROBLEM SOLVING. Using basic thinking processes to resolve a known or defined difficulty.

QUALIFICATION. Finding unique characteristics of particular identity or description.

REASONING. Has two forms: deductive and inductive; deductive—to use knowledge of two or more premises to infer if a conclusion is valid; inductive—to collect observations and formulate hypotheses based upon them.

RECALL. Remembrance of what has been learned or experienced.

RELATIONSHIPS. Detecting regular operations.

RULES. The principals that underlie some problems or relationships.

SEQUENCE. To arrange in a continuous or connected series based on a particular property or characteristic.

STRATEGY. The art of devising or employing plans toward a goal.

SYLLOGISM. Two or more premises that are used to derive valid conclusions.

SYNTHESIS. To put together or to form a composition or combination of parts so as to form a whole.

THINKING. The mental manipulation of sensory input to formulate thoughts, reason about, or judge.

TRANSFORMATION. Relating known to unknown characteristics, creating meanings.

VERTICAL THINKING. Thinking that is logical and straight-forward; used in the refinement and development of ideas; compare with lateral thinking.

From Thinking Skills: Meanings and Models, *by Barbara Z. Presseisen, in* Developing Minds: A Research Book for Teaching Thinking, *Arthur L. Costa, ed. (Alexandria, VA: Association for Supervision and Curriculum Development, 1985).*

BIBLIOGRAPHY

Ackoff, Russell L. *The Art of Problem Solving*. New York: John Wiley, 1978.

Adler, Mortimer J. *The Paideia Proposal: An Educational Manifesto*. New York: Macmillan, 1982.

Armbruster, Bonnie B., and Thomas H. Anderson. "Research Synthesis on Study Skills." *Educational Leadership* 39 (1981): 154-156.

Beilin, Harry. "The Psychology of Mathematics Learning." *Education and Urban Society* 17 (1985): 377-385.

Belmont, John M., Earl C. Butterfield, and Ralph P. Ferretti. "To Secure Transfer of Training Instruct Self-Management Skills." In *How and How Much Can Intelligence Be Increased*, edited by Douglas K. Detterman and Robert J. Sternberg, 147-154. Norwood, NJ: ABLEX, 1982.

Benderson, Albert. *Critical Thinking*. Focus 15. Princeton, NJ: Educational Testing Service, 1984.

Benderson, Albert. "Growing Up Is Hard to Do." *ETS Developments* 31 (1985): 5-8.

Bereiter, Carl. "How to Keep Thinking Skills from Going the Way of All Frills." *Educational Leadership* 42 (1984): 75-77.

Berman, Louise M. *New Priorities in the Curriculum*. Columbus, OH: Charles E. Merrill, 1968.

Berman, Louise M. "Perspectives and Imperatives: Re-searching, Rethinking, and Reordering Curriculum Priorities." *Journal of Curriculum and Supervision* 1 (1985): 66-71.

Berman, Paul, and Milbrey W. McLaughlin. *Federal Programs Supporting Educational Change*. Vol. 3, *Implementing and Sustaining Innovations*. R-1589/8-HEW. Santa Monica, CA: RAND Corporation, 1978.

Berrueta-Clement, John R., Lawrence J. Schweinhart, W. Steven Barnett, Ann
S. Epstein, and David P. Weikart. *Changed Lives: The Effects of the Perry
Preschool Program on Youths Through Age 19.* Ypsilanti, MI: High/Scope Press,
1984.

Beyer, Barry K. "Common Sense about Teaching Thinking Skills." *Educational
Leadership* 41 (1983): 44-49.

Beyer, Barry K. "What's in a Skill? Defining the Thinking Skills We Teach." *Social Science Review* 24 (1984): 19-23.

Beyer, Barry K. "Critical Thinking Revisited." *Social Education* 49 (1985): 268-302.

Beyer, Barry K. "Teaching Thinking Skills: How the Principal Can Know They
Are Being Taught." *NASSP Bulletin* 69 (1985): 70-83.

Billington, David P. Engineering and the Liberal Arts. An address at the presidential inauguration at Drexel University, Philadelphia, 27 April 1985.

Black, Howard, and Sandra Black. *Building Thinking Skills.* Book 1. Pacific Grove,
CA: Midwest Publications, 1984.

Bloom, Benjamin S. "Automaticity." *Educational Leadership* 43 (1986): 70-77.

Boehm, Anne E. *Boehm Test of Basic Concepts.* Form B, No. 23. New York:
The Psychological Corporation, 1971.

Bracey, Gerald W. "On the Compelling Need to go Beyond Minimum Competency." *Phi Delta KAPPAN* 64 (1983): 717-721.

Brandwein, Paul, Elizabeth K. Cooper, Paul E. Blackwood, Elizabeth B. Hone,
and Thomas P. Fraser. *Concepts in Science.* 3rd Edition. New York: Harcourt
Brace, 1972.

Brown, Ann L. "Teaching Students to Think as They Read: Implications for Curriculum Reform." Reading Education Report No. 58 (Washington, DC: National Institute of Child Health and Human Development, 1985).

Brown, John S. "Idea Amplifiers—New Kinds of Electronic Learning Environments." *educational HORIZONS* 63 (special edition, 1985): 108-112.

Bruner, Jerome S. *The Process of Education.* New York: Vintage Books, 1960.

Bruner, Jerome S. *On Knowing: Essays for the Left Hand.* New York: Atheneum,
1967.

Bruner, Jerome S. "Models of the Learner." *Educational Researcher* 14 (1985): 5-8.

Burns, Richard W., and Gary D. Brooks. "Processes, Problem Solving and Curriculum Reform." *Educational Technology* 10 (1970): 10-13.

Campione, Joseph C., and Bonnie B. Armbruster. "Acquiring Information from
Texts: An Analysis of Four Approaches." In *Thinking and Learning Skills.* Vol.
1. Edited by Judith W. Segal, Susan F. Chipman, and Robert Glaser. Hillsdale, NJ: Lawrence Erlbaum Associates, 1985.

Cassidy, Edward W., and Dana G. Kurfman. "Decision Making as Purpose and
Promise." In *Developing Decision-Making Skills.* 47th Yearbook. Edited by
Dana G. Kurfman, Washington, DC: National Council for the Social Studies,
1977.

Center for Performance Assessment. "Developing Good Tests: The 5x8 Card Makes It Easier." *Captrends* 10 (1985): 1-3.

Chall, Jeanne S. *Stages of Reading Development*. New York: McGraw-Hill, 1983.

Chance, Paul. *Thinking in the Classroom: A Survey of Programs*. New York: Basic Books, 1986.

Cohen, Jozef. *Thinking*. Chicago: Rand McNally, 1971.

The College Board. *Academic Preparation for College*. New York: College Board, 1983.

Conlin, David A., H.T. Fillmer, Ann Lefcourt, and Nell C. Thompson. *Our Language Today*. New York: American Book, 1970.

Cornbleth, Catherine. "Critical Thinking and Cognitive Process." In *Review of Research in Social Studies Education*. Bulletin 75. Edited by William B. Stanley, Catherine Cornbleth, R. K. Jantz, K. Klawitter, J. S. Leming, J. L. Nelson, J. P. Shaver, and J. L. White, 11-63. Boulder, CO: ERIC Clearinghouse for Social Studies/Social Science Education, 1985.

Costa, Arthur L. "Mediating the Metacognitive." *Educational Leadership* 42 (1984): 57-62.

Council for Economic Development. *Investing in Our Children*. New York: Committee for Economic Development, 1985.

Cyert, Richard M. "Problem Solving and Educational Processing." In *Problem Solving and Education: Issues in Teaching and Research*, edited by David T. Tuma and Frederick Reif. Hillsdale, NJ: Lawrence Erlbaum Associates, 1980.

Darling-Hammond, Linda. "Mad-Hatter Tests of Good Teaching." *New York Times*, 8 January 1984, p. 57.

Davis, Robert B. *Discovery in Mathematics: Student Discussion Guide*. Menlo Park, CA: Addison Wesley, 1964.

deBono, Edward. "The CoRT Thinking Program." In *Thinking and Learning Skills*. Vol. 1. Edited by Judith W. Segal, Susan F. Chipman, and Robert Glaser. Hillsdale, NJ: Lawrence Erlbaum Associates, 1985.

Dewey, John. *Experience in Education*. London: Collier-Macmillan, 1938.

Dorr-Bremme, Donald W. "Assessing Students: Teachers' Routine Practices and Reasoning." *Evaluation Comment* 8 (1983): 1-12.

Ecenbarger, William. "The Amazing Story of the Faber Pencil." *Philadelphia Inquirer Magazine*, 16 June 1985, 15-19.

Eisner, Elliot W. "Creative Education in American Schools Today." *educational HORIZONS* 63 (special edition, 1985): 10-15.

Elkind, David. "The View of David Elkind." In *The Development of Adolescent Thinking: Some Views for Effective Schools*. Edited by Barbara Z. Presseisen, 23-28. Philadelphia: Research for Better Schools, 1983.

Ennis, Robert H. *Goals for a Critical-Thinking/Reasoning Curriculum*. Champaign, IL: Illinois Thinking Project, 1984.

Ennis, Robert H. "Critical Thinking and the Curriculum." *National Forum* 65 (1985): 28-31.

Epstein, Leslie. "Atrocity and Imagination." *Harpers* 271 (1985): 13-16.

Fair, Jean. "Skills in Thinking." In *Developing Decision-Making Skills*. 47th Yearbook. Edited by Dana G. Kurfman. Washington, DC: National Council for the Social Studies, 1977.

Feldman, David H. "Piaget on Giftedness—A Very Short Essay." *The Genetic Epistemologist* 12 (1983): 1-10.

Feldman, David H. "The Child as Craftsman." *Thinking* 6 (1985): 20-24.

Feuerstein, Reuven, Mogens R. Jensen, Mildred B. Hoffman, and Yaacov Rand. "Instrumental Enrichment, an Intervention Program for Structural Cognitive Modifiability: Theory and Practice" In *Thinking and Learning Skills*. Vol. 1. Edited by Judith W. Segal, Susan F. Chipman, and Robert Glaser. Hillsdale, NJ: Lawrence Erlbaum Associates, 1985.

Flavell, John H. "Metacognitive Aspects of Problem Solving." In *The Nature of Intelligence*, edited by Lauren B. Resnick. Hillsdale, NJ: Lawrence Erlbaum Associates, 1976.

Frederiksen, Norman. "Implications of Cognitive Theory for Instruction in Problem Solving." *Review of Educational Research* 54 (1984): 363-407.

Gardner, Howard. *Frames of Mind: The Theory of Multiple Intelligences*. New York: Basic Books, 1983.

Gardner, Howard. *The Mind's New Science*. New York: Basic Books, 1985.

Ginsburg, Herbert. *Children's Arithmetic: How They Learn It and How You Teach It*. Austin, TX: Pro-Ed, 1982.

Glaser, Robert. "Education and Thinking: The Role of Knowledge." *American Psychologist* 39 (1984): 93-104.

Gordon, Ira J. *Studying the Child in School*. New York: John Wiley, 1966.

Halpern, Diane F. *Thought and Knowledge: An Introduction to Critical Thinking*. Glossary. Hillsdale, NJ: Lawrence Erlbaum Associates, 1984.

Hechinger, Fred M. "Making 'A Lot of Words' Tell a Story." *New York Times*, 10 September 1985, p. C7.

Hilton, Thomas L. *National Changes in Spatial-Visual Ability from 1960-1980*. Princeton, NJ: Educational Testing Service: 1985.

Hirsch, Eric D., "Cultural Literacy and the Schools." *American Educator* 9 (1985): 8-15.

Honig, Bill. "The Educational Excellence Movement: Now Comes the Hard Part." *Phi Delta KAPPAN* 66 (1985): 675-681.

"How to Clone an Expert." *Time*, 2 September 1985, p. 44.

Hunkins, Francis P. "A Systematic Model for Curriculum Development." *NASSP Bulletin* 69 (1985): 23-27.

Jones, Beau F., Minda Amiran, and Michael Katims. "Teaching Cognitive Strategies and Text Structures Within Language Arts Programs." In *Thinking and*

Learning Skills. Vol. 1. Edited by Judith W. Segal, Susan F. Chipman, and Robert Glaser. Hillsdale, NJ: Lawrence Erlbaum Associates, 1985.

Kamii, Constance. "Autonomy: The Aim of Education Envisioned by Piaget." *Phi Delta KAPPAN* 65 (1984): 410-415.

Kaplan, George R. *Items for an Agenda: Educational Research and the Reports on Excellence.* Washington, DC: American Educational Research Association, 1985.

Kaplan, Justine. "New Terrain in College Math." *New York Times*, 14 April 1985, section 12, p. 23.

Karplus, Robert. *Science Curriculum Improvement Study: Relative Position and Motion.* Chicago: Rand McNally, 1967.

Kirst, Michael W., and Gail R. Meister. "Turbulence in American Secondary Schools: What Reforms Last?" *Curriculum Inquiry* 15 (1985): 169-186.

Kitchener, Karen S. "Cognition, Metacognition, and Epistemic Cognition: A Three-Level Model of Cognitive Processing." *Human Development* 26 (1983): 222-232.

Klauer, Karl J. "Framework for a Theory of Teaching." *Teaching and Teacher Education* 1 (1985): 5-17.

Klausmeier, Herbert J., James M. Lipham, and John C. Daresh. *The Renewal and Improvement of Secondary Education: Concepts and Practices.* New York: University Press of America, 1983.

Klein, M. Frances. "The Use of a Research Model to Guide Curriculum Development." *Theory Into Practice* 22 (1983): 198-202.

Kneedler, Pete. *A Practical Workshop on the Critical Thinking Skills in Social Studies.* Sacramento, CA: California Assessment Program, 1984.

Kottmeyer, William, and Audrey Claus. *Basic Goals in Spelling.* 4th ed. New York: Webster Division, McGraw-Hill, n.d.

Kurfman, Dana G., ed. *Developing Decision-Making Skills.* 47th Yearbook. Washington, DC: National Council for the Social Studies, 1977.

Langer, William L., ed. *An Encyclopedia of World History.* Boston: Houghton Mifflin, 1956.

Larkin, Jill H. "Teaching Problem Solving in Physics: The Psychological Laboratory and the Practical Classroom." In *Problem Solving and Education: Issues in Teaching and Research*, edited by David T. Tuma and Frederick Reif, 111-115. Hillsdale, NJ: Lawrence Erlbaum Associates, 1980.

Leighton, Robert. "Gone but Not Forgotten." *Games Magazine* 9 (1985): 40.

Lieberman, Ann. "The Curriculum Reform Debate: Some Critical Issues." *Teacher's College Record* 85 (1984): 663-670.

Link, Frances, ed. *Essays on the Intellect.* Alexandria, VA: Association for Supervision and Curriculum Development, 1985.

Lochhead, Jack. "Research Synthesis on Problem Solving." *Educational Leadership* 39 (1981): 68-70.

Lochhead, Jack. "New Horizons in Educational Development." In *Review of Research in Education.* Vol. 12. Edited by Edmund W. Gordon, 3-9. Washington, DC: American Educational Research Association, 1985.

Lochhead, Jack. "Teaching Analytic Reasoning Skills Through Pair Problem Solving." In *Thinking and Learning Skills.* Vol. 1. Edited by Judith W. Segal, Susan F. Chipman, and Robert Glaser, 109-131. Hillsdale, NJ: Lawrence Erlbaum Associates, 1985.

Macdonald, James B. "The Person in the Curriculum." In *Precedents and Promise in the Curriculum Field,* edited by Helen F. Robinson, 38-52. New York: Teachers College Press, 1966.

Maeroff, Gene I. "Student Reading Held Its Level for 14 Years, Federal Survey Finds." *New York Times,* 19 September 1985, p. A16.

McKean, Kevin. "Intelligence: New Ways to Measure the Wisdom of Man." *Discover* 6 (1985): 25-41.

Moise, Edwin E., and Floyd L. Downs. *Geometry.* Menlo Park, CA: Addison Wesley, 1975.

National Science Board Commission. *Educating Americans for the 21st Century: A Plan of Action for Improving Mathematics, Science and Technology Education for All American Elementary and Secondary Students so That Their Achievement Is the Best in the World by 1995.* Washington, DC: National Science Board Commission on Precollegiate Education in Mathematics, Science and Technology, National Science Foundation, 1983.

Nicely, Robert F., Jr. "Higher-Order Thinking Skills in Mathematics Textbooks." *Educational Leadership* 42 (1985): 26-30.

Nickerson, Raymond S. "Thoughts on Teaching Thinking." *Educational Leadership* 39 (1981): 21-24.

Nickerson, Raymond S., W. Salter, S. Shepard, and J. Herrnstein. *The Teaching of Learning Strategies.* Cambridge, MA: Bolt, Beranek and Newman, 1984.

Olson, Carol B. "Fostering Critical Thinking Skills Through Writing." *Educational Leadership* 42 (1984): 28-39.

Olson, David R. "What is Worth Knowing and What Can Be Taught?" *School Review* 82 (1973): 27-43.

Olson, David R. "Culture, Technology, and Intellect." In *The Nature of Intelligence,* edited by Lauren B. Resnick, 189-202. Hillsdale, NJ: Lawrence Erlbaum Associates, 1976.

Olson, David R. "Computers as Tools of the Intellect." *Educational Researcher* 14 (1985): 5-7.

Olson, Lynn. "Reading Skills Up But Leveling Off, Report Finds." *Education Week,* 25 September 1985, pp. 1, 17.

Osborn, Jean H., Beau F. Jones, and Marcy Stein. "The Case for Improving Textbooks." *Educational Leadership* 42 (1985): 9-16.

Paul, Richard W. "Critical Thinking: Fundamental to Education for a Free Society." *Educational Leadership* 42 (1984): 4-14.

Paul, Richard W. "The Critical Thinking Movement." *National Forum* 65 (1985): 2-3.

Perkins, David N. *The Mind's Best Work*. Cambridge, MA: Harvard University Press, 1983.

Perkins, David N. "Creativity by Design." *Educational Leadership* 42 (1984): 18-25.

Perkins, David N. "The Fingertip Effect: How Information Processing Technology Shapes Thinking." *Educational Researcher* 14 (1985): 11-17.

Piaget, Jean. In *Piaget's Theory in Carmichael's Manual of Child Psychology*. Vol. 1. Edited by Paul H. Mussen, 703-732. New York: John Wiley, 1970.

Pogrow, Stanley. "Helping Students to Become Thinkers." *Electronic Learning* 4 (1985): 26-29.

Pratt, David. *Curriculum Design and Development*. New York: Harcourt, Brace, Jovanovich, 1980.

Presseisen, Barbara Z., ed. *The Development of Adolescent Thinking: Some Views for Effective Schools*. Philadelphia: Research for Better Schools, 1983.

Presseisen, Barbara Z. "Thinking Skills: Meanings and Models." In *Developing Minds: A Resource Book for Teaching Thinking*, edited by Arthur L. Costa. Alexandria, VA: Association for Supervision and Curriculum Development, 1985.

Presseisen, Barbara Z. *Unlearned Lessons: Current and Past Reforms for School Improvement*. Philadelphia and London: Falmer Press, 1985.

Presseisen, Barbara Z. *Critical Thinking and Thinking Skills: State of the Art Definitions and Practice in Public Schools*. Philadelphia: Research for Better Schools, 1986.

Purkey, Stewart C. *School Improvement: An Analysis of an Urban School District Effective Schools Project*. Madison, WI: Wisconsin Center for Educational Research, 1984.

Purkey, Stewart C., and Susan Degen. "Beyond Effective Schools to Good Schools: Some First Steps." In *R&D Perspectives*. Eugene, OR: Center for Educational Policy and Management, University of Oregon, 1985.

Raudsepp, Eugene. "Profile of the Creative Individual." Part 1. *Creative Computing* 9 (1983): 170-179.

Raudsepp, Eugene. "Profile of the Creative Individual." Part 2. *Creative Computing* 9 (1983): 196-209.

Reif, Frederick. *Teaching Higher-Order Thinking Skills for a Technological World: Needs and Opportunities*. Washington, DC: National Institute of Education, 1984.

Resnick, Lauren B. "Changing Conceptions of Intelligence." Introduction to *The Nature of Intelligence*. New York: John Wiley, 1976.

Robinson, Virginia. *Making Do in the Classroom: A Report on the Misassignment of Teachers*. Washington, DC: Council for Basic Education and American Federation of Teachers, 1985.

Rubinstein, Moshe F. *Patterns of Problem Solving*. Englewood Cliffs, NJ: Prentice-Hall, 1975.

Salomon, Gavriel. *Interaction of Media, Cognition, and Learning*. San Francisco: Jossey-Bass, 1979.

Samson, Richard W. *Thinking Skills*. Stamford, CT: Innovative Sciences, 1975.

Scardamalia, Marlene. "Higher Order Abilities: Written Communication." Paper presented for the American Educational Research Association Project: Research Contributions for Educational Improvement, New Orleans, LA, 1984.

Schoenfeld, Alan H. "Can Heuristics Be Taught?" In *Cognitive Process Instruction: Research on Teaching Thinking Skills*, edited by Jack Lochhead and John Clement. Philadelphia: The Franklin Institute Press, 1979.

Schoenfeld, Alan H. "Teaching Problem-Solving Skills." *The American Mathematical Monthly* 87 (1980): 794-805.

Schoenfeld, Alan H. "Psychology and the Mathematical Method." *Education and Urban Society* 17 (1985): 387-403.

Schwebel, Milton. "The Clash of Cultures in Academe: The University and the Education Faculty." *Journal of Teacher Education* 36 (1985): 2-7.

Segal, Judith, Susan F. Chipman, and Robert Glaser, eds. *Thinking and Learning Skills*. Vol. 1. Hillsdale, NJ: Lawrence Erlbaum Associates, 1985.

Shane, Harold G. *A Study of Curriculum Content for the Future*. New York: The College Board, 1981.

Shulman, Lee, and Evan R. Keislar, eds. *Learning by Discovery: A Critical Appraisal*. Chicago: Rand McNally, 1966.

Simon, Herbert A. "Problem Solving and Education." In *Problem Solving and Education: Issues in Teaching and Research*, edited by David T. Tuma and Frederick R. Reif, 81-96. Hillsdale, NJ: Lawrence Erlbaum Associates, 1980.

Sizer, Theodore. *Horace's Compromise: The Dilemma of the American High School*. Boston: Houghton Mifflin, 1984.

Sloan, Douglas. "On Raising Critical Questions about the Computer in Education." *Teachers College Record* 85 (1984): 539-547.

Sternberg, Robert J. "The Nature of Mental Abilities." *American Psychologist* 34 (1979): 214-230.

Sternberg, Robert J. "Intelligence as Thinking and Learning Skills." *Educational Leadership* 39 (1981): 18-20.

Sternberg, Robert J. "How Can We Teach Intelligence?" *Educational Leadership* 42 (1984): 38-48.

Sternberg, Robert J. "Testing Intelligence Without I.Q. Tests." *Phi Delta KAPPAN* 65 (1984): 694-698.

Sternberg, Robert J. "What Should Intelligence Tests Test? Implications of a Triarchic Theory of Intelligence for Intelligence Testing." *Educational Researcher* 13 (1984): 5-15.

Sternberg, Robert J. *Intelligence Applied: Understanding and Increasing Intellectual Skills*. San Francisco: Harcourt, Brace & Jovanovich, 1985.

Stuart, John A., and Richard W. Burns. "The Thinking Process: A Proposed Instructional Objectives Classification Scheme." *Educational Technology* 24 (1984): 21-26.

Sylwester, Robert. "Research on Memory: Major Discoveries and Major Educational Challenges." *Educational Leadership* 42 (1985): 69-75.

Turkle, Sherry. *The Second Self: Computers and the Human Spirit.* New York: Simon and Schuster, 1984.

Walker, Decker F. "Reflections on the Educational Potential and Limitations of Microcomputers." *Phi Delta KAPPAN* 65 (1983): 103-107.

Wallower, Lucille, and Ellen J. Wholey. *All About Pennsylvania.* State College, PA: Penns Valley Publishing, 1971.

Walton, Susan, and Thomas Toch. "Competency Tests Linked to Decline in Analytic Skills." *Education Week*, 8 December 1982, pp. 1, 17.

Whimbey, Arthur. "The Key to Higher Order Thinking Is Precise Processing." *Educational Leadership* 42 (1984): 66-70.

Whimbey, Arthur, and Linda S. Whimbey. *Intelligence Can Be Taught.* New York: E.P. Dutton, 1975.

Wick, John W., and Jeffrey K. Smith. *Developing Cognitive Abilities Test: Teacher's Manual.* Glenview, IL: Scott, Foresman, 1980.

Wirtz, Robert W. *Individualized Computation.* Vol. d1. Washington, DC: Curriculum Development Associates, n.d.

Wood, Earl F. *Junior English Review Exercises.* Book 1. Cambridge, MA: Educator's Publishing Service, 1979.

Worsham, Antoinette, and Anita Stockton. *A Model for Teaching Thinking Skills: The Inclusion Process.* Fastback No. 236. Bloomington, IN: Phi Delta Kappa, 1986.